Betty Crocker's

COOKING FOR TWO

PRENTICE HALL

NEW YORK   LONDON   TORONTO   SYDNEY   TOKYO   SINGAPORE

PRENTICE HALL
15 Columbus Circle
New York, New York 10023

PRENTICE HALL is a registered trademark and colophon is a trademark of Prentice-Hall, Inc.

BETTY CROCKER and BISQUICK are registered trademarks of General Mills, Inc.

Library of Congress Cataloging-in-Publication Data

Betty Crocker's cooking for two.
p.   cm.
Includes index.
ISBN 0-671-88827-7
1. Cookery for two.   I. Cooking for two.
TX652.B4973   1994
641.5′61—dc20   93-34241
                                                  CIP

Designed by Levavi & Levavi

Manufactured in the United States of America
10   9   8   7   6   5   4   3   2   1

First Edition

GENERAL MILLS, INC.
Betty Crocker Food and Publications Center
Director: Marcia Copeland
Editor: Jean E. Kozar
Recipe Development: Sheryl Heiken
Food Stylists: Kate Courtney Condon, Carol Grones
Nutrition Department
Nutritionist: Elyse A. Cohen, M.S.
Photographic Services
Photographer: Nancy Doonan Dixon

Cover: Honeyed Chicken Kabobs (page 11), Lemon Curd Parfaits (page 98), Cheesy Garlic Biscuit (page 66)
Back cover: Mushroom Quiches (page 104)

CONTENTS

Nutrition Information for Recipes

Each recipe in this book includes nutrition information Per Serving, which can be found at the end of each recipe. Besides calories, the nutrients calculated include protein, carbohydrate (including dietary fiber), fat (including unsaturated and saturated), cholesterol and sodium. The percentages of U.S. RDAs have also been calculated for Vitamins A and C, Calcium and Iron.

• If ingredient choices are given, such as "⅓ cup plain yogurt or sour cream," the first ingredient in the ingredient list was used to calculate the nutrition information.

• When a range is given for an ingredient, the first amount listed was used for nutrition calculation.

• Ingredients referred to as "if desired" are not included in the nutrition calculations, whether mentioned in the ingredient listing or in the recipe text as a suggestion.

• An asterisk (*) indicates that the recipe contains less than 2% U.S. RDA of that nutrient.

• For our recipe testing and nutrition calculations, large eggs, 2% milk and regular stick margarine and butter (not whipped) were used. No low-fat or nonfat ingredients were used.

INTRODUCTION

We've enjoyed creating this exciting new cookbook for the millions of smaller households in this country. Whether you are a young couple or older retirees, roommates or parent and child, you'll find that the delicious main-dish recipes in this book fit *your* life-style—no more complicated math to scale recipes down, and no more leftovers!

There are recipes here for every taste and every occasion. School-night suppers, romantic dinners and quick weekend lunches are easy and delicious. From casual Beef Burritos to traditional meat loaf, and elegant Cornish hen to festive Jambalaya, you'll find just about every recipe you need in this book—tailored just for two. And menu suggestions and special information boxes in each chapter make planning and cooking meals easier than ever.

When you don't have much time, you'll love our special chapter, "When Time Counts." All of the recipes in this chapter take 30 minutes or less to prepare. Just because you're short on time doesn't mean that you have to shortchange your meals. Go ahead and try the Italian Kabobs, Hot and Spicy Chile or Shrimp-Pasta Salad Toss—they're ready to eat in half an hour at most.

To round out the main-dish recipes, we've included a selection of salad, vegetable, bread and dessert recipes as a special feature in each of the first four chapters. And the special feature in the chapter "When Time Counts" gives even more great ideas on how to speed up your meal preparations. From main dishes to desserts, and old favorites to special new recipes, this book helps you make terrific meals for two anytime.

Enjoy!

—*The Betty Crocker Editors*

CHAPTER
(1)
▼▼▼▼▼▼▼ MENUS ▼▼▼▼▼▼

CONGRATULATORY DINNER
Peppered Chicken with Peanut Sauce
(page 7)
Couscous
Hot spinach with garlic
Sliced tomatoes
Berries with brown sugar and sour cream

✖

FARMER'S MARKET FARE
Chicken Fiesta (page 12)
Steamed baby carrots
Chocolate-dipped strawberries •
sugar cookies

✖

SPECIAL SCHOOL NIGHT SUPPER
Honeyed Chicken Kabobs (page 11)
Favorite gelatin salad
Cupcakes and ice cream

✖

JIGSAW PUZZLE NIGHT
Turkey with Mushrooms and Wine (page 14)
Fettuccine
Vegetable medley
Lemon Curd Parfaits (page 98)

THANKSGIVING DINNER
Hot spiced apple cider
Cornish Hen with Bulgur (page 12)
Maple-glazed Carrots and Apples (page 21)
Broccoli spears
Cranberry gelatin salad
Pumpkin pie with praline ice cream

✖

ANGLER'S SUPPER
Baked Fish with Honey-Lemon Sauce
(page 18)
Steamed new potatoes
Coleslaw
Cheesy Garlic Biscuits (page 66)
Apple pie with cheese

✖

LUNCH BY THE WATER
Dilled Salmon Salad (page 19)
Crisp bread sticks
Fresh fruit and cheese
Lemonade

✖

CELEBRATION DINNER
Garlic-Almond Shrimp (page 22)
Caesar salad
Chocolate-Toffee Torte (page 99)

C H A P T E R

1

POULTRY AND SEAFOOD

Peppered Chicken with Peanut Sauce

Couscous (which can be found shelved near the rice in your supermarket) is an easy alternative to rice and pasta. In just about 5 minutes you'll have the perfect accompaniment to this chicken.

> *2 skinless boneless chicken breast halves (about ½ pound)*
>
> *¼ teaspoon freshly ground pepper*
>
> *Salt*
>
> *1 tablespoon margarine or butter*
>
> *Peanut Sauce (right)*
>
> *1 tablespoon chopped fresh cilantro, if desired*

Sprinkle both sides of chicken breast halves with pepper; sprinkle lightly with salt. Heat margarine in 10-inch skillet over medium heat. Cook chicken in margarine 10 to 12 minutes, turning after 5 minutes, until juices are no longer pink when center of thickest piece is cut. Remove chicken from skillet; keep warm. Prepare Peanut Sauce in same skillet; serve over chicken. Sprinkle with cilantro. *2 servings.*

PEANUT SAUCE

> *¼ cup chopped red bell pepper*
>
> *¼ cup peanut butter*
>
> *½ cup water*
>
> *1 tablespoon lime juice*
>
> *¼ teaspoon ground coriander*
>
> *¼ teaspoon ground cumin*
>
> *1 green onion, sliced*
>
> *1 small clove garlic, chopped*

Mix all ingredients in 10-inch skillet. Heat over medium heat, stirring frequently, until hot and slightly thickened.

NUTRITION PER SERVING: Calories 390; Protein 34g; Carbohydrate 9g (Dietary Fiber 2g); Fat 25g (Unsaturated 20g, Saturated 5g); Cholesterol 65mg; Sodium 550mg.

PERCENT OF U.S. RDA: Vitamin A 16%; Vitamin C 22%; Calcium 4%; Iron 10%

Chicken Breasts with Orange Glaze

This delightfully fruity chicken is just as delicious when you use apricot, peach or pineapple preserves in the glaze instead of orange marmalade.

Orange Glaze (below)
2 skinless boneless chicken breast halves
(about ½ pound)
1 tablespoon margarine or butter, melted
Salt
Pepper

Prepare Orange Glaze; keep warm. Set oven control to broil. Brush chicken breast halves with half of the margarine. Place chicken on rack in broiler pan. Broil with tops 4 inches from heat about 4 minutes or until chicken just starts to brown. Sprinkle chicken lightly with salt and pepper. Turn chicken; brush with remaining margarine. Broil about 5 minutes longer or until chicken is brown and juices are no longer pink when center of thickest piece is cut. During the last 2 minutes of broiling, brush chicken with glaze. Heat any remaining glaze to boiling; serve with chicken. *2 servings.*

ORANGE GLAZE

½ teaspoon cornstarch
¼ teaspoon ground mustard
¼ cup orange juice
2 tablespoons orange marmalade
1 tablespoon soy sauce

Mix cornstarch and mustard in 1-cup container with tight lid. Add remaining ingredients. Cover and shake well to mix ingredients. Pour into 1-quart saucepan. Heat to boiling. Boil and stir about 1 minute or until thickened.

NUTRITION PER SERVING: Calories 260; Protein 27g; Carbohydrate 18g (Dietary Fiber 0g); Fat 9g (Unsaturated 7g, Saturated 2g); Cholesterol 65mg; Sodium 1180mg.

PERCENT OF U.S. RDA: Vitamin A 8%; Vitamin C 10%; Calcium 2%; Iron 8%

Chicken Amandine

To toast nuts, sprinkle them in ungreased heavy skillet. Cook over medium heat 4 to 6 minutes, stirring frequently until nuts begin to brown, then stirring constantly until golden brown.

3 tablespoons fine dry bread crumbs
3 tablespoons finely chopped toasted almonds
1 teaspoon chopped fresh or ¼ teaspoon dried savory leaves
2 skinless boneless chicken breast halves (about ½ pound)
2 tablespoons margarine or butter, melted

Heat oven to 375°. Grease square baking dish, 8×8×2 inches. Mix bread crumbs, almonds and savory in shallow bowl. Dip chicken breast halves in margarine, then coat with crumb mixture. Place in baking dish. Sprinkle with any remaining crumb mixture, and drizzle with any remaining margarine. Bake uncovered 20 to 25 minutes or until juices of chicken are no longer pink when center of thickest piece is cut. *2 servings.*

NUTRITION PER SERVING: Calories 345; Protein 30g; Carbohydrate 9g (Dietary Fiber 2g); Fat 22g (Unsaturated 18g, Saturated 4g); Cholesterol 65mg; Sodium 260mg.

PERCENT OF U.S. RDA: Vitamin A 16%; Vitamin C *%; Calcium 4%; Iron 12%

Chicken Italiano

½ pound skinless boneless chicken breast halves or turkey tenderloin

2 teaspoons olive or vegetable oil

1 ounce sliced pepperoni, cut into ¼-inch strips (about ¼ cup)

1 clove garlic, finely chopped

1 large bell pepper, cut into 1-inch squares

1 small onion, thinly sliced

1 small zucchini, cut into julienne strips

2 tablespoons dry red wine or chicken broth

½ teaspoon Italian seasoning

Dash of pepper

1 tablespoon grated Parmesan cheese

Cut chicken breast halves into 1-inch pieces. Heat oil in 10-inch skillet over medium-high heat. Add chicken, pepperoni and garlic; stir-fry 3 to 5 minutes or until outside of chicken is white. Remove chicken mixture from skillet; keep warm. Heat remaining ingredients except cheese to boiling in skillet; stir-fry 2 to 3 minutes or until vegetables are crisp-tender. Stir in chicken mixture; cook until chicken is no longer pink in center. Sprinkle with cheese. *2 servings.*

NUTRITION PER SERVING: Calories 285; Protein 30g; Carbohydrate 10g (Dietary Fiber 2g); Fat 15g (Unsaturated 11g, Saturated 4g); Cholesterol 75mg; Sodium 400mg.

PERCENT OF U.S. RDA: Vitamin A 6%; Vitamin C 44%; Calcium 8%; Iron 12%

TAILORED FOR TWO
Quick-to-Fix Chicken

This is an easy way to have chicken on hand, ready to cook. Several "batches" can be made up in minutes for the freezer.

Place two boneless skinless chicken breast halves (about ½ pound) in 1-quart labeled, sealable, heavy-duty plastic freezer bag.

Press all air out of bag to reduce freezer burn; seal. Refrigerate 8 to 24 hours or freeze up to 2 months.

To prepare, cook thawed chicken according to one of the methods below. (If frozen, place chicken in the refrigerator the night before you plan to use it, or in the morning before you leave for work.)

On Top of the Stove	*Broiling*	*Grilling*	*Microwaving*
Heat 1 teaspoon oil in 10-inch nonstick skillet over medium heat. Add chicken. Cook 8 to 10 minutes, turning once, or until golden brown and juice of chicken is no longer pink when centers of thickest pieces are cut.	Place chicken on rack in broiler pan. Broil 4 to 6 inches from heat 8 to 10 minutes, turning once, until juice is no longer pink when centers of thickest pieces are cut.	Grill 4 to 5 inches from medium coals 10 to 15 minutes, turning once, until juice is no longer pink when centers of thickest pieces are cut.	Place on microwavable plate. Cover with waxed paper and microwave on High 3 to 5 minutes, rotating plate ½ turn after 2 minutes. Let stand 3 minutes.

Chicken Paprikash

Serve Chicken Paprikash with a fresh spinach salad and whole wheat muffins. You'll love this hearty meal.

2 skinless boneless chicken breast halves (about ½ pound)

1 tablespoon vegetable oil

1 tablespoon margarine or butter

½ medium onion, cut into thin wedges

1 teaspoon paprika

½ cup chicken broth

1 teaspoon chopped fresh or ¼ teaspoon dried thyme leaves

⅓ cup plain yogurt or sour cream

2 teaspoons all-purpose flour

2 cups hot cooked noodles

Flatten chicken breast halves to ¼-inch thickness between plastic wrap or waxed paper. Heat oil in 10-inch skillet over medium-high heat until hot. Cook chicken in oil about 4 minutes, turning once, until light brown on outside and no longer pink in center. Remove chicken from skillet; keep warm. Heat margarine in skillet over medium heat until melted. Cook onion and paprika in margarine about 2 minutes, stirring constantly, until onion is almost tender. Stir in broth and thyme. Heat to boiling.

Meanwhile, mix yogurt and flour. Gradually stir yogurt mixture into boiling broth mixture in skillet. Cook, stirring constantly, until thickened (do not boil). Return chicken to skillet. Cook 1 minute longer. Serve chicken and sauce over noodles. Sprinkle with chopped fresh parsley if desired. *2 servings.*

NUTRITION PER SERVING: Calories 400; Protein 34g; Carbohydrate 28g (Dietary Fiber 2g); Fat 18g (Unsaturated 14g, Saturated 4g); Cholesterol 95mg; Sodium 480mg.

PERCENT OF U.S. RDA: Vitamin A 16%; Vitamin C 2%; Calcium 10%; Iron 16%

Curry Chicken Sandwiches

(Photograph on page 34)

1 tablespoon margarine or butter, melted

¼ teaspoon lemon pepper

2 skinless boneless chicken breast halves (about ½ pound)

Salt

Pepper

1 tablespoon mayonnaise or salad dressing

1 tablespoon plain yogurt or sour cream

¼ teaspoon curry powder

2 lettuce leaves

2 kaiser rolls or hamburger buns, split

Set oven control to broil. Mix margarine and lemon pepper. Brush chicken breast halves with half of the margarine mixture. Place chicken on rack in broiler pan. Broil with tops 4 inches from heat about 4 minutes or until chicken just starts to brown. Sprinkle lightly with salt and pepper. Turn chicken; brush with remaining margarine mixture. Broil about 5 minutes longer or until chicken is brown on outside and juices are no longer pink when center of thickest piece is cut.

Meanwhile, mix mayonnaise, yogurt and curry powder. Place lettuce leaf on bottom of each roll. Place chicken on lettuce. Top with dollop of mayonnaise mixture and tops of rolls. *2 servings.*

NUTRITION PER SERVING: Calories 390; Protein 32g; Carbohydrate 31g (Dietary Fiber 2g); Fat 16g (Unsaturated 12g, Saturated 4g); Cholesterol 70mg; Sodium 1020mg.

PERCENT OF U.S. RDA: Vitamin A 10%; Vitamin C 2%; Calcium 6%; Iron 16%

Honeyed Chicken Kabobs

8 small new potatoes or 2 medium
   potatoes

¼ cup honey

3 tablespoons lime juice

2 teaspoons chopped fresh or ½ teaspoon
   dried basil leaves

2 skinless boneless chicken breast halves
   (about ½ pound)

½ medium bell pepper

Pierce or peel narrow strip from around center of each new potato, or cut each medium potato into 4 pieces. Heat 1 inch water (salted if desired) to boiling in 1½-quart saucepan. Add potatoes. Cover and heat to boiling; reduce heat. Boil 15 minutes. Drain well.

Set oven control to broil. Mix honey, lime juice and basil. Cut each chicken breast half lengthwise into 4 strips. Cut bell pepper into 8 pieces. Thread 2 chicken strips, 2 potato pieces and 2 pepper pieces alternately on each of four 11-inch skewers,* leaving space between each piece. Place kabobs on rack in broiler pan. Brush some of the honey mixture over kabobs.

Broil kabobs with tops about 4 inches from heat about 5 minutes or until chicken is brown; turn. Brush with some of the honey mixture. Broil 4 to 5 minutes longer or until chicken is golden brown on outside and no longer pink in center. Heat remaining honey mixture to boiling; serve with kabobs. *2 servings.*

* If using bamboo skewers, soak in water at least 30 minutes before using to prevent burning.

NUTRITION PER SERVING: Calories 410; Protein 29g; Carbohydrate 67g (Dietary Fiber 3g); Fat 4g (Unsaturated 3g, Saturated 1g); Cholesterol 65mg; Sodium 75mg.

PERCENT OF U.S. RDA: Vitamin A 2%; Vitamin C 30%; Calcium 4%; Iron 16%

Chicken and Cheese-Tortellini Soup

For a taste of Italy, substitute Italian seasoning for the marjoram.

½ pound skinless boneless chicken breast
   halves

1 medium carrot, sliced (about ½ cup)

2 to 3 medium green onions, sliced (about
   ¼ cup)

½ cup cubed parsnip

3 cups chicken broth

1 teaspoon chopped fresh or ¼ teaspoon
   dried marjoram leaves

3 ounces uncooked refrigerated or frozen
   (thawed) cheese-filled tortellini (about
   ½ cup)

2 tablespoons grated Parmesan cheese

Cut chicken into 1-inch pieces. Heat chicken, carrot, onions, parsnip, broth and marjoram to boiling in 2-quart saucepan; reduce heat. Cover and simmer about 15 minutes, stirring occasionally, until chicken is no longer pink in center and vegetables are almost tender.

Stir in tortellini. Heat to boiling; reduce heat. Simmer uncovered about 5 minutes, stirring occasionally, until tortellini are tender. Sprinkle with cheese. *2 servings.*

NUTRITION PER SERVING: Calories 340; Protein 42g; Carbohydrate 21g (Dietary Fiber 3g); Fat 11g (Unsaturated 7g, Saturated 4g); Cholesterol 130mg; Sodium 1430mg.

PERCENT OF U.S. RDA: Vitamin A 52%; Vitamin C 8%; Calcium 16%; Iron 18%

Chicken Fiesta

(Photograph on page 33)

Tailor this easy main dish to your taste by trying the many kinds of picante sauces and salsas now available.

> *½ pound skinless boneless chicken breast halves*
>
> *1 tablespoon margarine or butter*
>
> *1 small zucchini, sliced (about 1 cup)*
>
> *½ cup sliced mushrooms (about 1½ ounces)*
>
> *1¼ cups picante sauce or salsa*
>
> *1 teaspoon sugar*
>
> *2 corn muffins, split*

Cut chicken into 1-inch pieces. Heat margarine in 10-inch skillet over medium heat until melted. Cook chicken in margarine 2 minutes, stirring constantly. Stir in zucchini and mushrooms. Cook, stirring frequently, until chicken is no longer pink in center and vegetables are tender. Stir in picante sauce and sugar. Cook 5 minutes, stirring occasionally, or until hot. Serve chicken mixture over muffins. *2 servings.*

NUTRITION PER SERVING: Calories 425; Protein 33g; Carbohydrate 44g (Dietary Fiber 4g); Fat 15g (Unsaturated 10g, Saturated 5g); Cholesterol 90mg; Sodium 1970mg.

PERCENT OF U.S. RDA: Vitamin A 24%; Vitamin C 10%; Calcium 16%; Iron 24%

Cornish Hen with Bulgur

(Photograph on page 37)

> *Bulgur-Bacon Stuffing (right)*
>
> *1 Rock Cornish hen (about 1½ pounds)*
>
> *1 tablespoon margarine or butter, melted*

Prepare Bulgur-Bacon Stuffing. Heat oven to 350°. Fill body cavity of hen with stuffing. Fasten opening with skewer. Place hen, breast side up, on rack in shallow roasting pan. Place meat thermometer in thigh muscle so tip does not touch bone. Brush hen with some of the margarine. Bake uncovered 1 to 1¼ hours, brushing occasionally with remaining margarine, until thermometer reads 180° and juices are no longer pink when center of thigh is cut. Remove stuffing from body cavity. Cut hen in half along backbone from tail to neck with kitchen scissors. Serve each hen half with stuffing. *2 servings.*

BULGUR-BACON STUFFING

> *1 slice bacon, chopped*
>
> *1 small onion, chopped (about ¼ cup)*
>
> *¼ cup water*
>
> *1 teaspoon chicken bouillon granules*
>
> *3 tablespoons uncooked bulgur*
>
> *¼ cup shredded zucchini*
>
> *¼ cup chopped mushrooms*
>
> *1 tablespoon dried cranberries or cherries, if desired*
>
> *½ teaspoon chopped fresh or ⅛ teaspoon dried thyme leaves*

Cook bacon and onion in 1-quart saucepan over medium-high heat, stirring frequently, until bacon is cooked and onion is tender. Drain bacon and onion. Heat water and bouillon granules to boiling in same saucepan. Stir in bulgur; remove from heat. Cover and let stand 15 minutes. Stir in bacon mixture, zucchini, mushrooms, cranberries and thyme.

NUTRITION PER SERVING: Calories 480; Protein 47g; Carbohydrate 19g (Dietary Fiber 4g); Fat 26g (Unsaturated 19g, Saturated 7g); Cholesterol 135mg; Sodium 870mg.

PERCENT OF U.S. RDA: Vitamin A 12%; Vitamin C 2%; Calcium 6%; Iron 18%

Gingered Turkey with Fruit

½ pound turkey tenderloin

1 teaspoon grated gingerroot or ½ teaspoon ground ginger

¼ teaspoon ground coriander

⅛ teaspoon ground allspice

1 cup chicken broth

½ cup pitted prunes, cut into fourths

¼ cup dried apricot halves, cut into halves

2 cups hot cooked rice

Heat oven to 350°. Cut turkey tenderloin into 1-inch cubes. Mix turkey, gingerroot, coriander, allspice and broth in 1½-quart casserole. Cover and bake 30 minutes. Stir in prunes and apricots. Cover and bake 15 to 20 minutes longer or until turkey is no longer pink in center. Stir before serving. Serve over rice. *2 servings.*

NUTRITION PER SERVING: Calories 550; Protein 32g; Carbohydrate 93g (Dietary Fiber 5g); Fat 8g (Unsaturated 5g, Saturated 3g); Cholesterol 70mg; Sodium 1240mg.

PERCENT OF U.S. RDA: Vitamin A 20%; Vitamin C 2%; Calcium 6%; Iron 32%

TAILORED FOR TWO
Pleasing Poultry

When cooking for two, you can't beat the availability and variety provided by poultry. Whether it's whole Cornish game hens, turkey breast slices, or boneless skinless chicken breasts, you'll find that smaller amounts (less than a pound) are readily available. Also check your store for canned or frozen cooked poultry.

What to Look for When Buying Fresh

• Plump and meaty pieces with smooth, moist-looking skin. Boneless, skinless cuts should look plump and moist, too.

• The cut ends of the bones should be pink to red in color; if gray, it is not as fresh.

• Avoid poultry that has traces of feathers or an off-odor.

How Much to Buy Per Serving

• Bone-in chicken—about ½ pound

• Boneless chicken—about 4 ounces

• One serving = 1 chicken breast half; 1 thigh; 2 legs; or 3 wings

When Is Poultry Done?

• Bone-in and Boneless Pieces: when juice is no longer pink when centers of thickest pieces are cut.

• Small Pieces (as for stir-fry, fajitas or chicken tenders): when no longer pink in center.

• Ground: when no longer pink.

How Should Poultry Be Stored?

• Uncooked pieces—Refrigerate tightly covered in original package 1 to 2 days. Freeze tightly wrapped up to 9 months; thaw in refrigerator.

• Cooked—Refrigerate tightly covered 1 to 2 days. Freeze tightly wrapped up to 1 month; thaw in refrigerator.

Turkey with Mushrooms and Wine

(Photograph on page 35)

For a hearty meal, serve over wild rice or other rice blend.

> *2 teaspoons margarine or butter*
>
> *1 small clove garlic, finely chopped*
>
> *½ pound boneless turkey breast slices or turkey tenderloin, ¼ to ½ inch thick*
>
> *Salt*
>
> *⅓ cup dry red wine or beef broth*
>
> *1 tablespoon tomato paste*
>
> *3 cups sliced mushrooms (about 8 ounces)*
>
> *1 green onion, chopped, if desired*

Heat margarine and garlic in 10-inch skillet over medium heat until hot. Sprinkle turkey breast slices lightly with salt. Cook turkey in margarine 8 to 10 minutes, turning once, until no longer pink in center. Remove turkey from skillet; keep warm.

Mix wine and tomato paste in skillet. Stir in mushrooms. Cook uncovered 3 to 5 minutes, stirring occasionally, until mushrooms are tender. Serve mushroom mixture over turkey. Sprinkle with onion. *2 servings.*

Note: If turkey pieces are more than ½ inch thick, flatten between plastic wrap or waxed paper.

NUTRITION PER SERVING: Calories 220; Protein 29g; Carbohydrate 8g (Dietary Fiber 2g); Fat 8g (Unsaturated 6g, Saturated 2g); Cholesterol 65mg; Sodium 710mg.

PERCENT OF U.S. RDA: Vitamin A 8%; Vitamin C 6%; Calcium 2%; Iron 16%

Oriental Turkey Stir-fry

To cut carrots on the diagonal, hold your knife at a 45° angle rather than at the usual 90° angle.

> *¼ cup chicken broth*
>
> *2 tablespoons dry sherry or water*
>
> *2 tablespoons soy sauce*
>
> *2 teaspoons cornstarch*
>
> *½ pound turkey breast slices*
>
> *1 tablespoon vegetable oil*
>
> *1 clove garlic, finely chopped*
>
> *1 tablespoon vegetable oil*
>
> *2 medium carrots, cut diagonally into thin slices (about 1 cup)*
>
> *1 cup Chinese pea pods*
>
> *2 cups hot cooked rice*

Mix broth, sherry, soy sauce and cornstarch; reserve. Cut turkey breast slices into bite-size pieces.

Heat wok or 10-inch skillet over high heat until 1 or 2 drops of water bubble and skitter when sprinkled in wok. Add 1 tablespoon oil; rotate wok to coat side. Add turkey and garlic; stir-fry about 4 minutes or until turkey is no longer pink in center. Remove turkey mixture from wok.

Add 1 tablespoon oil to wok; rotate wok to coat side. Add carrots and pea pods; stir-fry 3 to 4 minutes or until carrots are crisp-tender. Stir in cornstarch mixture. Cook and stir until thickened. Stir in turkey mixture; heat through. Serve over rice. *2 servings.*

NUTRITION PER SERVING: Calories 465; Protein 34g; Carbohydrate 46g (Dietary Fiber 4g); Fat 18g (Unsaturated 14g, Saturated 4g); Cholesterol 65mg; Sodium 1600mg.

PERCENT OF U.S. RDA: Vitamin A 94%; Vitamin C 32%; Calcium 8%; Iron 24%

Turkey-Pineapple Salad

(Photograph on page 36)

To make pineapple "boats," just cut a pineapple in half lengthwise and remove the fruit. Save half for another use and cut the remainder into chunks for the salad.

½ pound turkey breast slices

1 tablespoon vegetable oil

1 cup cauliflowerets

2 to 3 medium green onions, sliced diagonally (about ¼ cup)

½ medium red bell pepper, cut into strips

2 cups bite-size pieces lettuce

1 can (15 ounces) pineapple chunks in juice, drained and 2 tablespoons juice reserved

1 tablespoon white wine vinegar or white vinegar

¼ teaspoon freshly ground pepper

Cut turkey breast slices into ½-inch pieces. Heat wok or 10-inch skillet over high heat until 1 or 2 drops of water bubble and skitter when sprinkled in wok. Add oil; rotate wok to coat side. Add cauliflowerets; stir-fry about 3 minutes or until crisp-tender. Add onions and bell pepper; stir-fry 1 minute. Remove vegetable mixture from wok. Add turkey to wok; stir-fry about 4 minutes or until no longer pink in center. Remove turkey from wok.

Toss lettuce, pineapple chunks, vegetable mixture and turkey in large salad bowl. Shake reserved pineapple juice, the vinegar and pepper in tightly covered container. Pour over turkey mixture; toss to coat. *2 servings.*

NUTRITION PER SERVING: Calories 330; Protein 29g; Carbohydrate 35g (Dietary Fiber 6g); Fat 11g (Unsaturated 9g, Saturated 2g); Cholesterol 65mg; Sodium 75mg.

PERCENT OF U.S. RDA: Vitamin A 26%; Vitamin C 100%; Calcium 8%; Iron 18%

Turkey-Pasta Salad

This main-dish salad also is delicious when made with tuna. Just use a 6-ounce can of tuna packed in water, drained, instead of the turkey.

¾ cup uncooked shell macaroni

½ pound turkey breast slices

1 tablespoon vegetable oil

¼ cup plain yogurt or sour cream

2 tablespoons mayonnaise or salad dressing

1 tablespoon chopped fresh chives or green onion tops

2 teaspoons Dijon mustard

1 small carrot, shredded (about ½ cup)

½ small cucumber, chopped (about ½ cup)

Cook macaroni as directed on package; drain. Meanwhile, cut turkey breast slices into bite-size pieces. Heat wok or 10-inch skillet over high heat until 1 or 2 drops of water bubble and skitter when sprinkled in wok. Add oil; rotate wok to coat side. Add turkey; stir-fry about 4 minutes or until no longer pink in center. Drain on paper towels.

Toss macaroni, turkey, carrot and cucumber in large bowl. Mix remaining ingredients; fold into macaroni mixture. Cover and refrigerate at least 2 hours. Stir in small amount of milk before serving if desired. *2 servings.*

NUTRITION PER SERVING: Calories 515; Protein 35g; Carbohydrate 44g (Dietary Fiber 2g); Fat 23g (Unsaturated 19g, Saturated 4g); Cholesterol 75mg; Sodium 420mg.

PERCENT OF U.S. RDA: Vitamin A 44%; Vitamin C 8%; Calcium 10%; Iron 18%

Caribbean Swordfish

(*Photograph on page 38*)

Peach Salsa (below)

2 swordfish, shark or other medium-fat fish steaks, 1 inch thick (about ¾ pound)

1½ teaspoons grated lime peel

2 tablespoons lime juice

2 tablespoons grapefruit juice

¼ teaspoon salt

1 small clove garlic, crushed

Prepare Peach Salsa; cover and refrigerate. Place fish steaks in ungreased loaf dish, 8½×4½×2½ inches. Mix remaining ingredients; pour over fish. Cover and refrigerate at least 2 hours, turning fish once.

Set oven control to broil. Spray broiler pan rack with nonstick cooking spray. Remove fish from marinade; reserve marinade. Place fish on rack in broiler pan. Broil with tops about 4 inches from heat about 16 minutes, turning and brushing with marinade after 8 minutes, until fish flakes easily with fork. Serve with salsa. *2 servings.*

PEACH SALSA

1 cup chopped fresh or frozen (thawed) peaches

2 tablespoons finely chopped red bell pepper

1 tablespoon finely chopped green onion

1 to 2 tablespoons grapefruit juice

2 teaspoons chopped fresh cilantro

Dash of salt

Mix all ingredients.

NUTRITION PER SERVING: Calories 225; Protein 27g; Carbohydrate 15g (Dietary Fiber 2g); Fat 7g (Unsaturated 5g, Saturated 2g); Cholesterol 80mg; Sodium 500mg.

PERCENT OF U.S. RDA: Vitamin A 12%; Vitamin C 28%; Calcium 2%; Iron 6%

Spanish Fish Rolls

1 can (8 ounces) pizza sauce

1 small onion, chopped (about ¼ cup)

⅓ cup water

2 tablespoons canned chopped green chiles

½ teaspoon sugar

¾ cup cooked rice

2 flounder or other lean fish fillets (about ½ pound)

2 tablespoons shredded Cheddar cheese

Heat pizza sauce, onion, water, chiles and sugar in 1-quart saucepan over medium heat about 3 minutes, stirring occasionally, until hot.

Heat oven to 350°. Stir ⅓ cup of the pizza sauce mixture into rice. Place half of the rice mixture on end of each fish fillet. Roll up each fillet; secure with toothpicks. Place fish rolls in ungreased pie plate, 9×1¼ inches. Pour remaining pizza sauce mixture over fish rolls. Cover with aluminum foil and bake 15 to 20 minutes or until fish flakes easily with fork. Sprinkle with cheese. *2 servings.*

NUTRITION PER SERVING: Calories 280; Protein 25g; Carbohydrate 29g (Dietary Fiber 2g); Fat 8g (Unsaturated 5g, Saturated 3g); Cholesterol 65mg; Sodium 710mg.

PERCENT OF U.S. RDA: Vitamin A 10%; Vitamin C 22%; Calcium 8%; Iron 10%

Broccoli-Sole Pinwheels

Serve these pinwheels right out of the custard cups. Or, run a knife around the edges and remove.

1 cup fresh or frozen broccoli cuts

¼ cup shredded carrot

2 tablespoons fine dry bread crumbs

2 tablespoons grated Parmesan cheese

1 egg yolk, beaten

2 sole or other lean fish fillets (about ½ pound)

1 tablespoon fine dry bread crumbs

1 tablespoon grated Parmesan cheese

1 teaspoon chopped fresh or ¼ teaspoon dried marjoram leaves

2 teaspoons margarine or butter, melted

Heat oven to 350°. Heat 1 inch water (salted if desired) to boiling in 1-quart saucepan. Add broccoli and carrot. Cover and heat to boiling; reduce heat. Simmer 5 minutes; drain well. Mix broccoli mixture, 2 tablespoons bread crumbs, 2 tablespoons cheese and the egg yolk. Place half of the broccoli mixture on end of each fish fillet. Roll up each fillet; secure each with 2 toothpicks. Lightly grease two 10-ounce custard cups. Using a very sharp knife, cut each fish roll into halves.

Carefully place 2 fish rolls, cut sides up, in each custard cup, pressing to make even. Cover with aluminum foil and bake 10 minutes.

Meanwhile, mix 1 tablespoon bread crumbs, 1 tablespoon cheese and the marjoram in small bowl. Stir in margarine. Sprinkle bread crumb mixture over fish pinwheels. Bake uncovered 5 to 10 minutes longer or until fish flakes easily with fork and crumb topping is golden. *2 servings.*

NUTRITION PER SERVING: Calories 230; Protein 26g; Carbohydrate 11g (Dietary Fiber 2g); Fat 10g (Unsaturated 6g, Saturated 4g); Cholesterol 165mg; Sodium 360mg.

PERCENT OF U.S. RDA: Vitamin A 38%; Vitamin C 34%; Calcium 16%; Iron 8%

Orange Roughy with Fruit and Walnuts

If orange roughy is not available in your supermarket, use perch, cod or haddock instead.

2 tablespoons vegetable oil

2 orange roughy or other lean fish fillets (about ½ pound)

1 tablespoon margarine or butter

2 tablespoons coarsely chopped walnuts

1½ teaspoons cornstarch

¼ teaspoon salt

⅓ cup chicken broth

⅓ cup orange juice

1½ teaspoons chopped fresh or ½ teaspoon dried basil leaves

1 can (11 ounces) mandarin orange segments, drained

1 kiwifruit, peeled and sliced

2 cups hot cooked rice

Heat oil in 10-inch skillet over medium heat until hot. Cook fish fillets in oil about 8 minutes, carefully turning once, until fish flakes easily with fork. Remove fish from skillet; keep warm. Drain oil from skillet.

Heat margarine in same skillet over medium heat until melted. Cook walnuts in margarine, stirring frequently, until golden. Remove walnuts from skillet. Stir cornstarch and salt into margarine remaining in skillet. Stir in broth, orange juice and basil. Heat to boiling, stirring constantly. Boil and stir 1 minute. Carefully stir in orange segments and kiwifruit until coated. Spoon sauce over fish. Sprinkle with walnuts. Serve with rice. *2 servings.*

NUTRITION PER SERVING: Calories 765; Protein 30g; Carbohydrate 95g (Dietary Fiber 4g); Fat 31g (Unsaturated 26g, Saturated 5g); Cholesterol 75mg; Sodium 1310mg.

PERCENT OF U.S. RDA: Vitamin A 10%; Vitamin C 74%; Calcium 12%; Iron 26%

Ginger Fish Stir-fry

½ pound halibut, tuna, monkfish or
  swordfish steaks

⅓ cup water

2 tablespoons soy sauce

1 teaspoon cornstarch

½ teaspoon sesame oil

1 tablespoon vegetable oil

½ teaspoon finely chopped gingerroot

1 cup sliced mushrooms (about 3 ounces)

1 cup fresh or frozen (thawed) asparagus
  cuts

1 cup shredded cabbage

1 tablespoon vegetable oil

2 cups hot cooked rice

Remove any skin and bone from fish steaks. Cut fish into 1-inch pieces. Mix water, soy sauce, cornstarch and sesame oil; reserve. Heat wok or 10-inch skillet over high heat until 1 or 2 drops of water bubble and skitter when sprinkled in wok. Add 1 tablespoon vegetable oil; rotate wok to coat side. Add gingerroot; stir-fry about 30 seconds or until gingerroot is light brown. Add mushrooms, asparagus and cabbage; stir-fry about 3 minutes or until vegetables are crisp-tender. Remove vegetable mixture from wok.

Add 1 tablespoon vegetable oil to wok; rotate wok to coat side. Add fish; stir-fry gently about 3 minutes, without breaking fish pieces, until fish flakes easily with fork. Carefully remove fish from wok. Stir cornstarch mixture; add to wok. Heat to boiling. Boil about 30 seconds or until thickened. Return fish and vegetable mixture to wok. Stir carefully to coat with sauce. Serve with rice. *2 servings.*

NUTRITION PER SERVING: Calories 390; Protein 24g; Carbohydrate 38g (Dietary Fiber 3g); Fat 17g (Unsaturated 14g, Saturated 3g); Cholesterol 50mg; Sodium 1510mg.

PERCENT OF U.S. RDA: Vitamin A 6%; Vitamin C 26%; Calcium 6%; Iron 14%

Baked Fish with Honey-Lemon Sauce

Next time you grill salmon steaks, spoon some of this Honey-Lemon Sauce over them—delicious!

2 haddock or other lean fish steaks (about
  ½ pound)

1 teaspoon lemon juice

1 tablespoon margarine or butter

2 green onions, sliced

1 tablespoon honey

¼ teaspoon finely shredded lemon peel

2 teaspoons lemon juice

½ teaspoon ground mustard

Heat oven to 450°. Grease square baking dish, 8×8×2 inches. Place fish steaks in baking dish. Drizzle with 1 teaspoon lemon juice. Bake uncovered 10 to 12 minutes or until fish flakes easily with fork.

Meanwhile, heat margarine in 1-quart saucepan over medium-high heat until melted. Cook onions in margarine about 2 minutes, stirring frequently, until tender. Stir in remaining ingredients. Heat 1 minute, stirring constantly, until well mixed and hot. Spoon over fish. *2 servings.*

NUTRITION PER SERVING: Calories 180; Protein 19g; Carbohydrate 10g (Dietary Fiber 0g); Fat 7g (Unsaturated 6g, Saturated 1g); Cholesterol 55mg; Sodium 150mg.

PERCENT OF U.S. RDA: Vitamin A 8%; Vitamin C 2%; Calcium 2%; Iron 2%

Dilled Salmon Salad

(Photograph on page 39)

Canned salmon is a quick and tasty substitute for the fresh salmon. Just use one 8-ounce can, drained (discard skin and bones), instead of the fresh salmon and chicken broth.

> *½ pound salmon steaks*
>
> *2 cups chicken broth*
>
> *1 small zucchini, sliced (about 1 cup)*
>
> *¼ cup sliced radishes*
>
> *¼ cup mayonnaise or salad dressing*
>
> *2 tablespoons ranch dressing*
>
> *1 teaspoon chopped fresh or ¼ teaspoon dried dill weed*
>
> *3 cups bite-size pieces spinach or other salad greens*

Place fish steaks and broth in 10-inch skillet. Heat to boiling; reduce heat. Simmer uncovered 5 to 10 minutes or until fish flakes easily with fork. Remove fish to platter. When fish is cool enough to handle, break into bite-size pieces, discarding skin and bones.

Mix salmon, zucchini and radishes in large bowl. Mix mayonnaise, ranch dressing and dill weed; fold into salmon mixture. Cover and refrigerate at least 2 hours. Serve salmon mixture on spinach or toss before serving. *2 servings.*

NUTRITION PER SERVING: Calories 450; Protein 29g; Carbohydrate 8g (Dietary Fiber 3g); Fat 35g (Unsaturated 29g, Saturated 6g); Cholesterol 60mg; Sodium 1180mg.

PERCENT OF U.S. RDA: Vitamin A 76%; Vitamin C 56%; Calcium 16%; Iron 22%

Tarragon Fish Chowder

Serve this rich chowder with a crisp tossed salad and crusty French bread, and you've got a perfect winter meal.

> *½ pound cod or other lean fish fillets*
>
> *1½ cups chicken broth*
>
> *1 small onion, chopped (about ¼ cup)*
>
> *¼ cup sliced celery*
>
> *¼ cup shredded carrot*
>
> *¾ teaspoon chopped fresh or ¼ teaspoon dried tarragon leaves*
>
> *⅛ teaspoon pepper*
>
> *1 bay leaf*
>
> *1 cup milk*
>
> *½ cup sour cream*
>
> *1 tablespoon all-purpose flour*

Cut fish fillets into bite-size pieces. Mix fish, broth, onion, celery, carrot, tarragon, pepper and bay leaf in 1½-quart saucepan. Heat to boiling; reduce heat. Cover and simmer 2 to 3 minutes or until fish flakes easily with fork and vegetables are tender. Stir in milk; heat through. Mix sour cream and flour; stir into milk mixture. Cook, stirring constantly, just until mixture starts to bubble (do not boil). Immediately remove from heat; remove bay leaf. *2 servings.*

NUTRITION PER SERVING: Calories 315; Protein 29g; Carbohydrate 15g (Dietary Fiber 1g); Fat 16g (Unsaturated 7g, Saturated 9g); Cholesterol 100mg; Sodium 760mg.

PERCENT OF U.S. RDA: Vitamin A 38%; Vitamin C 4%; Calcium 24%; Iron 6%

VEGETABLE BOUNTY

Getting your 3 to 5 servings of vegetables each day can seem daunting at times—but don't worry, it's easier than you think! Just be sure to try interesting vegetable combinations and tantalizing flavors. These tempting recipes for two will certainly top your list of side-dish favorites.

Curried Asparagus

(*Photograph on page 46*)

You can also use fresh or frozen whole asparagus, and top the hot asparagus with the sauce and peanuts.

> *1½ cups fresh asparagus cuts**
> *1 small onion, chopped (about ¼ cup)*
> *¼ cup sour cream or plain yogurt*
> *¼ teaspoon curry powder*
> *2 tablespoons chopped salted peanuts*

Heat 1 inch water (salted if desired) to boiling in 1-quart saucepan. Add asparagus and onion. Heat to boiling; reduce heat. Simmer uncovered 3 minutes. Cover and simmer about 4 minutes longer or until crisp-tender; drain.

Heat sour cream and curry powder in same saucepan, stirring constantly, until warm; fold into asparagus. Sprinkle with peanuts. *2 servings.*

* Frozen asparagus cuts can be substituted for the fresh asparagus. Cook as directed on package, adding onion; drain.

NUTRITION PER SERVING: Calories 140; Protein 6g; Carbohydrate 10g (Dietary Fiber 3g); Fat 10g (Unsaturated 6g, Saturated 4g); Cholesterol 20mg; Sodium 50mg.

PERCENT OF U.S. RDA: Vitamin A 10%; Vitamin C 10%; Calcium 6%; Iron 4%

Sweet-and-Sour Vegetable Stir-fry

Serve these colorful vegetables with roast pork or broiled pork chops.

> *1 tablespoon vegetable oil*
> *½ cup sliced yellow summer squash or zucchini*
> *½ cup sliced mushrooms (about 1½ ounces)*
> *4 green onions, cut diagonally into 1-inch pieces*
> *½ cup Chinese pea pods*
> *3 tablespoons prepared sweet-and-sour sauce*
> *1 tablespoon water*

Heat wok or 10-inch skillet over high heat until 1 or 2 drops of water bubble and skitter when sprinkled in wok. Add oil; rotate wok to coat side. Add squash, mushrooms and onions; stir-fry about 3 minutes or until vegetables are crisp-tender. Add pea pods; stir-fry about 1 minute or until pea pods are crisp-tender. Stir in sweet-and-sour sauce and water. Cook and stir about 1 minute or until mixture is heated through. *2 servings.*

NUTRITION PER SERVING: Calories 125; Protein 3g; Carbohydrate 15g (Dietary Fiber 3g); Fat 7g (Unsaturated 6g, Saturated 1g); Cholesterol 0mg; Sodium 80mg.

PERCENT OF U.S. RDA: Vitamin A 2%; Vitamin C 20%; Calcium 4%; Iron 12%

Maple-glazed Carrots and Apples

(Photograph on page 37)

2 medium carrots, sliced (about 1 cup)
1 tablespoon margarine or butter
1 medium apple, cut into thin wedges
2 tablespoons maple-flavored syrup
¼ teaspoon ground cardamom

Heat 1 inch water (salted if desired) to boiling in 1-quart saucepan. Add carrots. Cover and heat to boiling; reduce heat. Simmer 12 to 15 minutes or until tender; drain.

Heat margarine in 6-inch skillet over medium heat until hot. Cook apple wedges in margarine 2 minutes, stirring occasionally. Stir in syrup and cardamom. Cook 3 to 5 minutes, stirring frequently, until apples are evenly glazed. Stir into carrots. *2 servings.*

NUTRITION PER SERVING: Calories 180; Protein 1g; Carbohydrate 33g (Dietary Fiber 3g); Fat 6g (Unsaturated 5g, Saturated 1g); Cholesterol 0mg; Sodium 135mg.

PERCENT OF U.S. RDA: Vitamin A 100%; Vitamin C 4%; Calcium 2%; Iron 2%

Sesame Vegetable Medley

(Photograph on page 21)

1½ cups frozen mixed broccoli, corn and
*   peppers*
1 tablespoon margarine or butter
2 teaspoons sesame seed
2 teaspoons lemon juice
¼ teaspoon finely shredded lemon peel

Cook frozen vegetables as directed on package; drain. Heat margarine in 10-inch skillet over medium heat until melted. Cook sesame seed in margarine about 5 minutes, stirring frequently, until golden brown; remove from heat. Stir in lemon juice and lemon peel; fold into vegetables. *2 servings.*

NUTRITION PER SERVING: Calories 95; Protein 3g; Carbohydrate 8g (Dietary Fiber 3g); Fat 7g (Unsaturated 6g, Saturated 1g); Cholesterol 0mg; Sodium 105mg.

PERCENT OF U.S. RDA: Vitamin A 86%; Vitamin C 20%; Calcium 4%; Iron 4%

Creamy Peas and Corn

¾ cup fresh or frozen peas
¾ cup frozen whole kernel corn
¼ cup soft-style cream cheese
1 teaspoon chopped fresh or ¼ teaspoon
*   dried dill weed*
¼ teaspoon lemon pepper

Heat 1 inch water (salted if desired) to boiling in 1-quart saucepan. Add peas and corn. Cover and heat to boiling; reduce heat. Simmer about 5 minutes or just until vegetables are tender; drain. Stir remaining ingredients into vegetables in saucepan. Cook 1 to 2 minutes, stirring occasionally, until cream cheese is melted. *2 servings.*

NUTRITION PER SERVING: Calories 145; Protein 6g; Carbohydrate 20g (Dietary Fiber 5g); Fat 7g (Unsaturated 3g, Saturated 4g); Cholesterol 20mg; Sodium 105mg.

PERCENT OF U.S. RDA: Vitamin A 10%; Vitamin C 4%; Calcium 2%; Iron 6%

Garlic-Almond Shrimp

(Photograph on page 40)

*½ pound fresh or frozen raw medium
 shrimp (in shells)*

1 cup boiling water

1 cup sliced mushrooms (about 3 ounces)

½ cup uncooked regular long grain rice

1 small onion, thinly sliced

1 clove garlic, finely chopped

½ teaspoon salt

½ teaspoon ground ginger

½ cup whole almonds, toasted

*1 can (11 ounces) mandarin orange
 segments, drained*

*1 package (6 ounces) frozen Chinese pea
 pods, thawed and drained*

Soy sauce, if desired

Peel shrimp. (If shrimp are frozen, do not thaw; peel in cold water.) Make a shallow cut lengthwise down back of each shrimp; wash out vein. Heat oven to 350°. Mix water, mushrooms, rice, onion, garlic, salt, ginger and shrimp in ungreased square baking dish, 8×8×2 inches. Cover tightly with aluminum foil and bake 35 to 40 minutes or until liquid is absorbed and shrimp are pink.

Stir in remaining ingredients except soy sauce. Cover and let stand 3 minutes or until pea pods are hot. Serve with soy sauce. *2 servings.*

NUTRITION PER SERVING: Calories 570; Protein 26g; Carbohydrate 78g (Dietary Fiber 9g); Fat 21g (Unsaturated 19g, Saturated 2g); Cholesterol 105mg; Sodium 670mg.

PERCENT OF U.S. RDA: Vitamin A 4%; Vitamin C 64%; Calcium 16%; Iron 42%

Crab and Wild Rice Soup

¼ cup uncooked wild rice

1¼ cups chicken broth

½ cup sliced leek

*1½ teaspoons chopped fresh or ½
 teaspoon dried oregano leaves*

Few dashes of red pepper sauce

1 tablespoon margarine or butter

1 tablespoon all-purpose flour

½ cup chicken broth

*1 cup cooked crabmeat or 1 package (6
 ounces) frozen crabmeat, thawed,
 drained and cartilage removed*

1 cup half-and-half

2 tablespoons chopped leek top

Place wild rice in wire strainer. Run cold water through rice, lifting rice with fingers to clean thoroughly. Heat wild rice, 1¼ cups broth, ½ cup leek, the oregano and pepper sauce to boiling in 1-quart saucepan, stirring once or twice; reduce heat. Cover and simmer 45 to 50 minutes, stirring occasionally, until wild rice is tender. (Mixture will be watery; do not drain.)

Heat margarine in 1½-quart saucepan over medium heat until melted. Stir in flour. Stir in wild rice mixture and ½ cup broth. Heat to boiling, stirring constantly. Boil and stir 1 minute.

Stir in crabmeat and half-and-half. Heat, stirring constantly, just until hot (do not boil). Sprinkle with 2 tablespoons leek top. *2 servings.*

NUTRITION PER SERVING: Calories 410; Protein 26g; Carbohydrate 29g (Dietary Fiber 2g); Fat 22g (Unsaturated 11g, Saturated 11g); Cholesterol 110mg; Sodium 990mg.

PERCENT OF U.S. RDA: Vitamin A 20%; Vitamin C 6%; Calcium 24%; Iron 12%

Scallops Mornay

¼ cup water or chicken broth

1 cup 1-inch cuts fresh asparagus or frozen (thawed) asparagus cuts

1 tablespoon margarine or butter

½ pound bay or sea scallops

1 tablespoon margarine or butter

1 tablespoon all-purpose flour

1 teaspoon chopped fresh or ¼ teaspoon dried chervil leaves

⅔ cup chicken broth

¾ cup shredded process Swiss cheese (3 ounces)

1 tablespoon dry sherry or chicken broth

2 cups hot cooked fettuccine or spinach fettuccine

Heat water to boiling in 1½-quart saucepan. Add asparagus. Heat to boiling; reduce heat. Simmer uncovered about 4 minutes, stirring occasionally, until crisp-tender; drain.

Heat 1 tablespoon margarine in same saucepan over medium-high heat until melted. Cook scallops in margarine 3 to 5 minutes, stirring frequently, until scallops are white. Remove scallops from saucepan. Drain liquid.

Heat 1 tablespoon margarine in same saucepan until melted. Stir in flour and chervil. Cook over medium heat, stirring constantly, until smooth and bubbly; remove from heat. Stir in broth. Heat to boiling, stirring constantly. Boil and stir 1 minute. Stir in cheese until melted. Stir in scallops, asparagus and sherry. Heat, stirring constantly, just until hot (do not boil). Serve scallop mixture over fettuccine. *2 servings.*

NUTRITION PER SERVING: Calories 585; Protein 45g; Carbohydrate 32g (Dietary Fiber 3g); Fat 32g (Unsaturated 20g, Saturated 12g); Cholesterol 100mg; Sodium 1000mg.

PERCENT OF U.S. RDA: Vitamin A 40%; Vitamin C 12%; Calcium 56%; Iron 30%

TAILORED FOR TWO
Sensational Seafood

Fish and shellfish come in many varieties and in several forms. For two, you'll probably find it easiest to purchase fillets and steaks.

What to Look for When Buying

• Flesh of fin fish should be firm and elastic; it should spring back when touched.

• Frozen fish should be tightly wrapped and frozen solid with little or no airspace between the packaging and the fish. Any discoloration may indicate freezer burn. Purchase fillets and steaks that are individually quick frozen so just 1 or 2 pieces (depending on the size) can be used at a time.

• There should be no off-odor.

How Much to Buy Per Serving

• Whole fish—about 1 pound

• Fish steaks (cross-sectional slices of large fish) and fillets (fleshy sides of fish, cut lengthwise)—4 ounces

• Shrimp—about ½ pound headless unpeeled or ¼ pound headless peeled shrimp

When Is Seafood Done?

• Fin fish: when fish flakes easily with fork or reaches 160°F using a meat thermometer

• Shellfish: when raw shrimp turns pink and firm; scallops turn white or opaque and become firm

How Should Seafood Be Stored?

• Uncooked—Refrigerate tightly covered in original package 1 to 2 days. Freeze in airtight container up to 4 months; thaw in refrigerator

• Cooked—Refrigerate tightly covered 1 to 2 days. Freeze tightly wrapped up to 2 months; thaw in refrigerator

CHAPTER

② MENUS

WEEKNIGHT FEAST
Mushroom-stuffed Steak au Poivre
(page 26)
Hurry-Up Potato Salad (page 52)
Sliced tomatoes
Baked apples with cream

✖

WEEKEND BRUNCH
Mixed fresh fruit
Confetti Corned Beef Hash (page 30)
Soft-cooked eggs
Muffins

✖

SPRING PLANTING DINNER
Meatballs with Cucumber-Mint Sauce
(page 28)
Rice
Steamed asparagus
Mediterranean Bread Crisps (page 67)
Lemon meringue pie

✖

BIKING THROUGH THE PARK
Pork with Chipotle Sauce (page 32)
Steamed green beans
Tossed salad with black beans and corn
Pineapple-Yogurt Shortcake (page 98)

COUNTRY DANCING NIGHT OUT
Spiced Orange Ribs (page 51)
Baked sweet potatoes
Creamy Peas and Corn (page 21)
Tossed salad
Frozen raspberry yogurt with hot fudge
sauce

✖

STARVED AFTER SHOPPING
Spicy Italian Soup (page 55)
Lettuce wedge with Italian dressing
Hard rolls
Spumoni or chocolate ice cream • Amaretto
cookies

✖

TENNIS LUNCH
Warm Black Bean and Sausage Salad
(page 55)
Tex-Mex Corn Muffins (page 67)
Iced tea

✖

BISTRO DINNER
Lamb Chops with Fruited Rice (page 57)
Curried Asparagus (page 20)
Pita or cracker bread
Lemon sherbet • Crisp cookies

CHAPTER 2
BEEF, PORK AND LAMB

Saucy Dill Steaks

(Photograph on page 41)

For a more piquant flavor, use 2 teaspoons of chopped fresh cilantro in place of the parsley.

1 tablespoon margarine or butter

2 tablespoons chopped onion

3 tablespoons grated Parmesan cheese

1 teaspoon all-purpose flour

1 teaspoon chopped fresh or ¼ teaspoon dried dill weed

½ teaspoon ground mustard

⅛ teaspoon pepper

½ cup milk

½ pound beef boneless sirloin steak, 1 to 1½ inches thick

1 tablespoon chopped fresh parsley

Heat margarine in 1-quart saucepan over medium heat until melted. Cook onion in margarine about 3 minutes, stirring occasionally, until tender. Stir in cheese, flour, dill weed, mustard and pepper. Cook over medium heat, stirring constantly, until smooth and bubbly; remove from heat. Stir in milk. Heat to boiling, stirring constantly. Boil and stir 1 minute. Remove from heat; keep warm.

Set oven control to broil. Place beef steak on rack in broiler pan. Broil with top 3 to 4 inches from heat about 4 minutes for rare or 6 minutes for medium. Turn beef; broil 6 minutes longer for rare or 8 minutes longer for medium. Cut beef into halves. Pour sauce over beef. Sprinkle with parsley, if desired. *2 servings.*

NUTRITION PER SERVING: Calories 240; Protein 26g; Carbohydrate 5g (Dietary Fiber 0g); Fat 13g (Unsaturated 9g, Saturated 4g); Cholesterol 65mg; Sodium 280mg.

PERCENT OF U.S. RDA: Vitamin A 12%; Vitamin C 2%; Calcium 18%; Iron 12%

Mushroom-stuffed Steak au Poivre

½ pound beef boneless top sirloin steak, 1½ inches thick

½ to ¾ teaspoon freshly cracked pepper

1 tablespoon margarine or butter

¾ cup sliced mushrooms (about 2 ounces)

2 medium green onions, sliced

1 clove garlic, finely chopped

Cut outer edge of fat on beef steak diagonally at 1-inch intervals to prevent curling (do not cut into meat). Sprinkle both sides of beef with pepper; press pepper into beef. Cut a deep horizontal slit in beef to form a pocket.

Heat margarine in 10-inch skillet over medium heat until melted. Cook mushrooms, onions and garlic in margarine, stirring frequently, until mushrooms are tender; remove from heat. Spoon mushroom mixture into pocket in beef. Close pocket opening by inserting 2 toothpicks in an X shape through edges of beef.

Set oven control to broil. Place beef on rack in broiler pan. Broil with tops 3 to 4 inches from heat about 6 minutes for rare or 8 minutes for medium. Turn beef; broil 5 minutes longer for rare or 7 minutes longer for medium. Remove toothpicks. Cut beef into halves. *2 servings.*

NUTRITION PER SERVING: Calories 175; Protein 22g; Carbohydrate 3g (Dietary Fiber 1g); Fat 9g (Unsaturated 7g, Saturated 2g); Cholesterol 55mg; Sodium 110mg.

PERCENT OF U.S. RDA: Vitamin A 8%; Vitamin C 2%; Calcium 2%; Iron 14%

Hearty Beef and Noodles

1 tablespoon margarine or butter

½ pound beef stew meat, cut into 1-inch pieces

1 clove garlic, finely chopped

2½ cups beef broth

1 medium carrot, sliced (about ½ cup)

¼ cup sliced celery

1 teaspoon chopped fresh or ¼ teaspoon dried marjoram leaves

1 teaspoon chopped fresh or ¼ teaspoon dried thyme leaves

⅛ teaspoon pepper

4 ounces refrigerated or frozen noodles

1 tablespoon red wine vinegar

Heat margarine in 3-quart saucepan over medium heat until melted. Cook beef and garlic in margarine about 6 minutes, stirring frequently, until beef is brown. Stir in broth, carrot, celery, marjoram, thyme and pepper. Heat to boiling; reduce heat. Cover and simmer about 45 minutes, stirring occasionally, until beef is almost tender.

Stir in noodles. Heat to boiling; reduce heat. Cover and simmer 20 to 25 minutes, stirring occasionally, until beef is tender and noodles are done. Stir in vinegar. Heat to boiling. *2 servings.*

NUTRITION PER SERVING: Calories 420; Protein 29g; Carbohydrate 44g (Dietary Fiber 4g); Fat 16g (Unsaturated 11g, Saturated 5g); Cholesterol 90mg; Sodium 940mg.

PERCENT OF U.S. RDA: Vitamin A 56%; Vitamin C 4%; Calcium 6%; Iron 28%

Stir-fried Beef and Vegetables

(Photograph on page 42)

Add frozen Chinese pea pods to the wok *after* the jicama strips and pepper pieces have cooked for about three minutes.

2 tablespoons soy sauce

2 tablespoons dry sherry or water

1 teaspoon sugar

½ pound beef top round steak

1 ounce cellophane noodles (bean threads), broken

1 tablespoon vegetable oil

2 teaspoons finely chopped gingerroot or 1 teaspoon ground ginger

2 cloves garlic, finely chopped

1 tablespoon vegetable oil

1 cup Chinese pea pods or 1 package (6 ounces) frozen (thawed) Chinese pea pods

1 cup julienne strips jicama or 1 medium onion, cut into thin wedges

1 small red or green bell pepper, cut into 1-inch pieces

Mix soy sauce, sherry and sugar; reserve. Trim fat from beef steak. Cut beef with grain into 2-inch strips. Cut strips across grain into ⅛-inch slices. (For ease in cutting, partially freeze beef about 1½ hours.) Soak noodles in enough warm water to cover for 15 minutes; drain.

Heat wok or 10-inch skillet over high heat until 1 or 2 drops of water bubble and skitter when sprinkled in wok. Add 1 tablespoon oil; rotate wok to coat side. Add beef, gingerroot and garlic; stir-fry about 3 minutes or until beef is no longer pink. Remove beef mixture from wok.

Add 1 tablespoon oil to wok; rotate wok to coat side. Add pea pods, jicama and bell pepper; stir-fry about 5 minutes or until vegetables are crisp-tender. Stir in beef mixture and noodles; heat to boiling. Stir in soy sauce mixture; cook and stir about 1 minute or until hot. *2 servings.*

NUTRITION PER SERVING: Calories 380; Protein 31g; Carbohydrate 26g (Dietary Fiber 3g); Fat 18g (Unsaturated 14g, Saturated 4g); Cholesterol 70mg; Sodium 1090mg.

PERCENT OF U.S. RDA: Vitamin A 14%; Vitamin C 76%; Calcium 6%; Iron 28%

Greek Beef with Couscous

1 tablespoon margarine or butter

1½ cups bite-size pieces cooked roast beef (about 6 ounces)

½ small red bell pepper, cut into strips

2 tablespoons chopped green onion

⅔ cup chicken broth

⅛ teaspoon pepper

⅓ cup uncooked couscous

2 tablespoons sliced almonds

1 tablespoon lemon juice

1 teaspoon chopped fresh or ½ teaspoon dried mint leaves

Heat margarine in 10-inch skillet over medium heat until melted. Cook beef, bell pepper and onion in margarine about 5 minutes, stirring occasionally, until vegetables are crisp-tender and beef is hot. Stir in broth and pepper; heat to boiling. Stir in couscous and almonds; remove from heat. Cover and let stand 5 minutes. Stir in lemon juice and mint. *2 servings.*

NUTRITION PER SERVING: Calories 535; Protein 34g; Carbohydrate 27g (Dietary Fiber 2g); Fat 33g (Unsaturated 22g, Saturated 11g); Cholesterol 85mg; Sodium 710mg.

PERCENT OF U.S. RDA: Vitamin A 14%; Vitamin C 20%; Calcium 4%; Iron 18%

Meat Loaf with Sweet-Sour Sauce

½ pound ground beef or pork

⅓ cup quick-cooking oats

¼ cup finely chopped onion

¼ cup finely chopped green bell pepper

2 tablespoons milk

½ teaspoon ground ginger

¼ teaspoon salt

1 egg

Sweet-Sour Sauce (below)

Heat oven to 350°. Mix all ingredients except Sweet-Sour Sauce. Spread mixture in ungreased loaf pan, 6×3×2 inches. Bake about 50 minutes or until meat loaf is no longer pink in center. Meanwhile, prepare Sweet-Sour Sauce. Remove meat loaf from pan. Serve sauce over meat loaf. *2 servings.*

SWEET-SOUR SAUCE

2 teaspoons cornstarch

¼ teaspoon garlic powder

¼ teaspoon ground mustard

½ cup cranberry juice cocktail

¼ cup barbecue sauce

Dash of red pepper sauce

Mix cornstarch, garlic powder and mustard in container with tight-fitting lid. Stir in remaining ingredients. Cover and shake well to combine ingredients. Transfer to a 1-quart saucepan. Heat to boiling. Boil and stir about 1 minute or until thickened.

NUTRITION PER SERVING: Calories 405; Protein 27g; Carbohydrate 29g (Dietary Fiber 2g); Fat 21g (Unsaturated 13g, Saturated 8g); Cholesterol 170mg; Sodium 620mg.

PERCENT OF U.S. RDA: Vitamin A 8%; Vitamin C 30%; Calcium 6%; Iron 18%

Meatballs with Cucumber-Mint Sauce

½ pound ground beef or pork

¼ cup fine dry bread crumbs

2 tablespoons finely chopped onion

2 tablespoons milk

¼ teaspoon salt

¼ teaspoon ground coriander

¼ teaspoon ground cumin

¼ teaspoon ground turmeric

¼ teaspoon paprika

1 egg, beaten

Cucumber-Mint Sauce (below)

Heat oven to 400°. Grease rectangular baking dish, 11×7×1½ inches. Mix all ingredients except Cucumber-Mint Sauce. Shape mixture into 12 balls. Place in baking dish. Bake uncovered about 20 minutes or until meatballs are no longer pink in center. Prepare Cucumber-Mint Sauce. Serve sauce over meatballs. *2 servings.*

CUCUMBER-MINT SAUCE

½ cup plain yogurt

¼ cup finely chopped seeded cucumber

1 teaspoon chopped fresh or ½ teaspoon dried mint leaves

Mix all ingredients. Cover and refrigerate until serving time.

NUTRITION PER SERVING: Calories 365; Protein 29g; Carbohydrate 16g (Dietary Fiber 1g); Fat 21g (Unsaturated 13g, Saturated 8g); Cholesterol 175mg; Sodium 490mg.

PERCENT OF U.S. RDA: Vitamin A 6%; Vitamin C 2%; Calcium 16%; Iron 18%

Beef Burritos

4 flour tortillas (10 inches in diameter)

½ pound ground beef or pork

1 small onion, chopped (about ¼ cup)

1 clove garlic, finely chopped

½ cup salsa

½ teaspoon ground cumin or chile powder

½ cup shredded Cheddar or hot pepper cheese (2 ounces)

Salsa

Shredded Cheddar cheese

Refrigerated or frozen (thawed) guacamole or avocado dip

Heat oven to 325°. Wrap tortillas in aluminum foil. Heat in preheating oven about 10 minutes or until warm. Remove tortillas from oven; keep wrapped.

Meanwhile, cook ground beef, onion and garlic in 10-inch skillet over medium heat about 5 minutes, stirring frequently, until beef is brown; drain. Stir in ½ cup salsa and the cumin.

Place ⅓ cup beef mixture on each tortilla, just below center. Top each with 2 tablespoons cheese. Fold bottom end of each tortilla up and over beef and cheese. Fold in opposite sides of each tortilla. Roll up tortillas from the bottom; secure with toothpicks. Place in ungreased square pan, 8×8×2 inches.

Cover with aluminum foil and bake 15 to 20 minutes or until heated. Remove toothpicks. Serve burritos on shredded lettuce if desired. Top with salsa, cheese and avocado dip. *2 servings.*

NUTRITION PER SERVING: Calories 690; Protein 33g; Carbohydrate 73g (Dietary Fiber 6g); Fat 32g (Unsaturated 18g, Saturated 14g); Cholesterol 90mg; Sodium 1600mg.

PERCENT OF U.S. RDA: Vitamin A 14%; Vitamin C 14%; Calcium 28%; Iron 41%

TAILORED FOR TWO
Marvelous Meats

Meats are leaner than ever before. It's especially important not to overcook muscle cuts of beef or pork, because the leaner meat is, the less tolerant it is of overcooking. Ground meats, steaks and chops are probably the easiest red meats to cook for two. Roasts are best when at least 2 pounds of meat is cooked, so you can cook a roast and then freeze the leftovers.

How Much to Buy Per Serving

• Boneless cuts (ground, boneless chops, loin, tenderloin)—about 4 ounces

• Bone-in cuts (steaks, chops, country-style ribs)—about 8 ounces

When Is Meat Done?

• Always cook ground beef patties to a minimum of medium doneness, at least 160°F on meat thermometer.

• Bone-in and boneless—use meat thermometer for most accurate doneness. Beef, rare (140°), medium (160°); Pork, medium (160°), well (170°).

How Should Meat Be Stored?

• Uncooked—Refrigerate ground meats tightly covered in original package 1 to 2 days. Keep chops and steaks up to 5 days. Freeze tightly wrapped up to 6 months; thaw in refrigerator.

• Cooked—Refrigerate tightly covered 1 to 2 days. Freeze tightly wrapped up to 3 months; thaw in refrigerator.

Spicy Beef Salad

*½ pound beef flank steak or boneless
sirloin steak*

2 tablespoons sherry

1½ teaspoons soy sauce

1 teaspoon sugar

2 to 3 medium green onions, thinly sliced

1 medium tomato, cut into chunks

2 cups sliced mushrooms (about 5 ounces)

*3 cups shredded lettuce (about ½ small
head) or radicchio (about 1 small head)*

Spicy Dressing (below)

Cut beef steak with grain into 2-inch strips. Cut strips across grain into ⅛-inch slices. (For ease in cutting, partially freeze beef about 1½ hours.) Toss beef, sherry, soy sauce and sugar in glass or plastic bowl. Cover and refrigerate 30 minutes.

Heat wok or 10-inch nonstick skillet over medium-high heat until 1 or 2 drops of water bubble and skitter when sprinkled in skillet. Add half of the beef; stir-fry about 3 minutes or until beef is no longer pink. Remove beef from skillet; drain. Repeat with remaining beef. Toss beef and onions in large bowl. Layer tomatoes, mushrooms and lettuce over beef. Cover and refrigerate at least 1 hour but no longer than 10 hours. Pour Spicy Dressing over salad; toss until well coated. *2 servings.*

SPICY DRESSING

*1 tablespoon rice wine vinegar or white
wine vinegar*

1 tablespoon soy sauce

½ teaspoon finely chopped gingerroot

½ teaspoon sesame oil

⅛ teaspoon ground red pepper (cayenne)

1 clove garlic, finely chopped

Shake all ingredients in tightly covered container.

NUTRITION PER SERVING: Calories 245; Protein 27g; Carbohydrate 14g (Dietary Fiber 2g); Fat 10g (Unsaturated 6g, Saturated 4g); Cholesterol 60mg; Sodium 850mg.

PERCENT OF U.S. RDA: Vitamin A 8%; Vitamin C 16%; Calcium 4%; Iron 22%

Confetti Corned Beef Hash

1 tablespoon margarine or butter

*1 cup chopped cooked potato (about 1
medium)*

*1 cup cut-up cooked corned beef or lean
cooked beef (about 4 ounces)*

1 tablespoon chopped fresh parsley

*½ teaspoon chopped fresh or ¼ teaspoon
dried thyme leaves*

½ small bell pepper, chopped

1 hard-cooked egg, chopped

1 medium green onion, sliced

Heat margarine in 10-inch nonstick skillet over medium heat. Stir in remaining ingredients. Cook uncovered 6 to 8 minutes, turning frequently, until hot. *2 servings.*

NUTRITION PER SERVING: Calories 320; Protein 17g; Carbohydrate 15g (Dietary Fiber 1g); Fat 22g (Unsaturated 16g, Saturated 6g); Cholesterol 175mg; Sodium 910mg.

PERCENT OF U.S. RDA: Vitamin A 14%; Vitamin C 26%; Calcium 4%; Iron 12%

Beef and Bean Soup

2 slices bacon

1 tablespoon vegetable oil

6 ounces beef stew meat, cut into 1-inch pieces

1 small onion, chopped (about ¼ cup)

1½ cups beef broth

½ cup dry white wine or beef broth

1 tablespoon chopped fresh or 1 teaspoon dried thyme leaves

¼ teaspoon pepper

1 bay leaf

1 can (15 to 16 ounces) navy, lima or great northern beans, rinsed and drained

2 medium carrots, cut into 1-inch pieces

1 medium stalk celery, cut into 1-inch pieces

Cook bacon in 1½-quart saucepan over medium heat until crisp; remove bacon and drain on paper towels. Crumble bacon and set aside. Heat oil in same skillet over medium-high heat until hot. Cook beef and onion in oil about 15 minutes, stirring frequently, until beef is brown.

Stir in broth, wine, thyme, pepper and bay leaf. Heat to boiling; reduce heat. Cover and simmer about 45 minutes, stirring occasionally, until beef is almost tender.

Stir in beans, carrots and celery. Cover and simmer about 30 minutes, stirring occasionally, until vegetables are tender. Remove bay leaf. Sprinkle bacon over each serving. Sprinkle with chopped fresh parsley if desired. *2 servings.*

NUTRITION PER SERVING: Calories 555; Protein 42g; Carbohydrate 68g (Dietary Fiber 18g); Fat 21g (Unsaturated 15g, Saturated 6g); Cholesterol 55mg; Sodium 1170mg.

PERCENT OF U.S. RDA: Vitamin A 100%; Vitamin C 12%; Calcium 20%; Iron 50%

Sour Cream–Onion Burgers

½ pound ground beef or pork

½ cup sour cream–and-onion dip

3 tablespoons fine dry bread crumbs

2 tablespoons chopped fresh parsley

⅛ teaspoon salt

⅛ teaspoon pepper

Leaf lettuce

2 hamburger buns, split and toasted

Sour cream–and-onion dip

Set oven control to broil. Mix ground beef, ½ cup sour cream dip, the bread crumbs, parsley, salt and pepper. Shape mixture into 2 patties, each about ¾ inch thick. Place patties on rack in broiler pan. Broil with tops about 3 inches from heat 14 to 16 minutes, turning once, until patties are no longer pink in center. Place lettuce leaf on bottom of each bun. Place patties on lettuce. Top with sour cream dip and tops of buns. *2 servings.*

NUTRITION PER SERVING: Calories 585; Protein 30g; Carbohydrate 42g (Dietary Fiber 2g); Fat 34g (Unsaturated 17g, Saturated 17g); Cholesterol 125mg; Sodium 1180mg.

PERCENT OF U.S. RDA: Vitamin A 8%; Vitamin C 6%; Calcium 20%; Iron 20%

Pork with Chipotle Sauce

Chipotle chiles are ripened, dried and smoked jalepeño chiles that can be purchased in specialty food shops or in the gourmet section of many supermarkets.

> Chipotle Sauce (*below*)
> ½ pound pork tenderloin, cut crosswise into 4 slices
> 1 tablespoon vegetable oil
> 1 small tomato, chopped (about ½ cup)
> 1 tablespoon sliced green onion top

Prepare Chipotle Sauce; keep warm. Flatten pork slices to ¼-inch thickness between plastic wrap or waxed paper. Heat oil in 10-inch skillet over medium-high heat until hot. Cook pork in oil 8 to 10 minutes, turning once, until no longer pink. Arrange on serving plate. Top with sauce. Sprinkle with tomato and onion. *2 servings.*

CHIPOTLE SAUCE

> ⅓ cup plain yogurt
> 1 medium green onion, chopped
> 1 canned chipotle chile in adobo sauce, drained, seeded and chopped (1 tablespoon)
> 1 tablespoon creamy peanut butter
> Dash of salt

Place all ingredients in blender. Cover and blend on medium speed about 20 seconds, stopping blender occasionally to scrape sides, until well blended. Heat sauce in 1-quart saucepan over low heat, stirring occasionally, until hot.

NUTRITION PER SERVING: Calories 325; Protein 37g; Carbohydrate 7g (Dietary Fiber 1g); Fat 17g (Unsaturated 13g, Saturated 4g); Cholesterol 110mg; Sodium 340mg.

PERCENT OF U.S. RDA: Vitamin A 4%; Vitamin C 10%; Calcium 8%; Iron 12%

Pork Chops with Tomato Relish

(*Photograph on page 43*)

> 1 small tomato, seeded and finely chopped (about ½ cup)
> 2 medium green onions, thinly sliced
> ¼ cup finely chopped seeded cucumber
> 3 tablespoons Russian dressing
> 2 teaspoons white vinegar
> ¾ teaspoon chopped fresh or ¼ teaspoon dried tarragon leaves
> ½ teaspoon prepared mustard
> 2 pork loin or rib chops (about ¾ pound), ¾ inch thick

Set oven control to broil. Mix tomato, onions and cucumber in small bowl. Mix dressing, vinegar, tarragon and mustard in separate small bowl. Stir half of the dressing mixture into tomato mixture. Cover and refrigerate tomato relish. Reserve remaining dressing mixture.

Cut outer edge of fat on pork chops diagonally at 1-inch intervals to prevent curling (do not cut into meat). Place pork on rack in broiler pan. Broil with tops about 4 inches from heat about 5 minutes or until brown. Turn pork; brush with dressing mixture. Broil 4 to 6 minutes longer for medium doneness (160°). Serve with tomato relish. *2 servings.*

NUTRITION PER SERVING: Calories 290; Protein 22g; Carbohydrate 6g (Dietary Fiber 1g); Fat 20g (Unsaturated 15g, Saturated 5g); Cholesterol 75mg; Sodium 270mg.

PERCENT OF U.S. RDA: Vitamin A 4%; Vitamin C 10%; Calcium 2%; Iron 6%

▲ *Chicken Fiesta* (Recipe on page 12)

▲ ***Turkey with Mushrooms and Wine*** (Recipe on page 14) and ***Sesame Vegetable Medley*** (Recipe on page 21)

◄ ***Curry Chicken Sandwiches*** (Recipe on page 10) and ***Hearty Lentil Soup*** (Recipe on page 73)

▲ *Cornish Hen with Bulgur* (Recipe on page 12) and *Maple-glazed Carrots and Apples* (Recipe on page 21)

◄ *Turkey-Pineapple Salad* (Recipe on page 15) and *Rich Herbed Rye Biscuits* (Recipe on page 66)

▲ *Dilled Salmon Salad* (Recipe on page 19) and *Orange Salad with Blackberry Dressing* (Recipe on page 52)

◄ *Caribbean Swordfish* (Recipe on page 16)

▲ *Saucy Dill Steaks* (Recipe on page 25)

◀ *Garlic-Almond Shrimp* (Recipe on page 22)

▲ *Pork Chops with Tomato Relish* (Recipe on page 32) and *Cheesy Garlic Biscuits* (Recipe on page 66)

◄ *Stir-fried Beef and Vegetables* (Recipe on page 27)

▲ *Country Bratwurst Chowder* (Recipe on page 56) and *Blueberry-Pear Crisps* (Recipe on page 98)

◄ *Fettuccine with Ham and Goat Cheese* (Recipe on page 54)

▲ *Dilled Fettuccine with Whiskey-Crab Sauce* (Recipe on page 60)

◄ *Lamb Chops with Fruited Rice* (Recipe on page 57) and *Curried Asparagus* (Recipe on page 20)

Mushroom Manicotti (Recipe on page 63) ▶

Marinated Pork Chops with Apple Stuffing

2 pork loin or rib chops (about 1 pound),
1¼ inches thick

¾ cup apple cider

1 tablespoon packed brown sugar

1 tablespoon cider vinegar

1½ teaspoons chopped fresh or ½
teaspoon dried tarragon leaves

1 clove garlic, finely chopped

2 tablespoons margarine or butter

¾ cup coarsely chopped apple

¼ cup chopped celery (with leaves)

1½ cups onion-flavored croutons

⅓ cup chicken broth

Salt

Pepper

Place pork chops in plastic bag or shallow glass dish. Mix apple cider, brown sugar, vinegar, tarragon and garlic; pour over pork. Fasten bag securely or cover dish with plastic wrap. Refrigerate at least 8 hours but no longer than 24 hours.

Heat oven to 350°. Remove pork from marinade. Cut a horizontal slit in each pork chop to form a pocket. Heat margarine in 1-quart saucepan over medium-high heat until melted. Cook apple and celery in margarine about 3 minutes, stirring frequently, until apple and celery are tender. Mix apple mixture, croutons and broth. Spoon about ¼ cup apple mixture into each pocket in pork chops. Close pocket openings by inserting 2 toothpicks in an X shape through edges of each pork chop. Place remaining apple mixture in greased 1-quart casserole; cover and set aside.

Place pork in ungreased shallow pan or baking dish, 8×8×2 inches. Bake uncovered 25 minutes.

Sprinkle lightly with salt and pepper; turn pork. Place covered casserole of stuffing in oven with pork. Bake about 20 minutes or until pork is medium doneness (160°) and stuffing is heated through. *2 servings.*

NUTRITION PER SERVING: Calories 435; Protein 22g; Carbohydrate 30g (Dietary Fiber 2g); Fat 26g (Unsaturated 15g, Saturated 11g); Cholesterol 55mg; Sodium 1200mg.

PERCENT OF U.S. RDA: Vitamin A 16%; Vitamin C 2%; Calcium 6%; Iron 10%

TAILORED FOR TWO
Vary Those Vegetables

Sometimes we get stuck in a rut and keep preparing the same two or three vegetables. Why not try some deliciously different vegetables?

• Take advantage of seasonal fresh vegetable specials at the supermarket or the farmer's market. Avoid vegetables with bruises or soft spots.

• Purchase enough vegetables for two and ask how to prepare them. Make a note of those you like and dislike—but try preparing them at least two different ways before you make a final judgement.

• Frozen vegetables come conveniently packaged for two. A 10-ounce package makes 2 or 3 servings. Buying the bags of individually quick-frozen vegetables allows you to remove only as much as is needed at a time.

• Frozen vegetables can be thawed only (not cooked) when used in cold pasta salads. Try some of the many combinations of mixed vegetables available.

• For variety, mix vegetables with rice as a side dish rather than eating each separately.

• Add herbs and seasonings to plain vegetables or toss with bottled salad dressings for a different twist.

Pork and Papaya Kabobs

Try beef boneless sirloin steak and mango instead of the pork loin and papaya for a delicious change of pace.

Lemon Rice (below)
½ pound pork boneless top loin
1 papaya, peeled
⅓ cup apricot preserves
1 tablespoon soy sauce
1 tablespoon dry sherry or water

Prepare Lemon Rice; keep warm. Cut pork loin into 1-inch cubes. Cut papaya into 1½-inch cubes. Heat preserves, soy sauce and sherry in 1-quart saucepan over medium heat, stirring occasionally, until preserves are melted.

Set oven control to broil. Grease broiler pan rack. Thread pork cubes alternately with papaya cubes on each of two 11-inch skewers,* leaving space between each piece. Place kabobs on rack in broiler pan. Brush kabobs generously with preserves mixture. Broil with tops about 3 inches from heat 6 minutes. Turn kabobs; brush generously with preserves mixture. Broil about 5 minutes longer or until pork is no longer pink in center. Serve over Lemon Rice. *2 servings.*

LEMON RICE

½ cup uncooked regular long grain rice
1 cup water
⅛ teaspoon salt
1 tablespoon chopped fresh parsley
1 tablespoon margarine or butter
1 tablespoon lemon juice

Heat rice, water and salt to boiling in 1-quart saucepan, stirring once or twice; reduce heat.

Cover and simmer 14 minutes. (Do not lift cover or stir.) Remove from heat. Fluff rice lightly with fork. Stir in parsley, margarine and lemon juice. Cover and let steam 5 to 10 minutes.

* If using bamboo skewers, soak in water at least 30 minutes before using to prevent burning.

NUTRITION PER SERVING: Calories 670; Protein 36g; Carbohydrate 87g (Dietary Fiber 5g); Fat 22g (Unsaturated 15g, Saturated 7g); Cholesterol 100mg; Sodium 830mg.

PERCENT OF U.S. RDA: Vitamin A 12%; Vitamin C 82%; Calcium 8%; Iron 18%

Moussaka

½ medium eggplant (about ½ pound),
  peeled
1 tablespoon margarine or butter, melted
Parmesan Cheese Sauce (right)
½ pound ground pork or lamb
1 small onion, chopped (about ¼ cup)
2 cloves garlic, finely chopped
¾ cup spaghetti sauce
½ teaspoon ground cinnamon
Ground cinnamon

Set oven control to broil. Cut eggplant into ¾-inch slices. Place on rack in broiler pan. Brush lightly with margarine. Broil with tops about 4 inches from heat about 3 minutes. Turn eggplant; brush lightly with margarine. Broil about 3 minutes longer or until tender. Meanwhile, prepare Parmesan Cheese Sauce.

Heat oven to 350°. Cook ground pork, onion and garlic in 10-inch skillet over medium heat about 5 minutes, stirring frequently, until pork is no longer pink; drain. Stir in spaghetti sauce and ½ teaspoon cinnamon.

Place half of the eggplant in 1-quart casserole. Spoon pork mixture over eggplant. Place remaining eggplant on pork mixture; pour sauce over top. Sprinkle with cinnamon. Bake uncovered about 30 minutes or until eggplant is tender in center. Let stand 10 minutes before serving. *2 servings.*

PARMESAN CHEESE SAUCE

1 tablespoon margarine or butter

1 tablespoon all-purpose flour

⅛ teaspoon salt

⅛ teaspoon pepper

1 cup milk

1 egg, slightly beaten

2 tablespoons grated Parmesan cheese

Heat margarine in 1-quart saucepan over medium heat until melted. Stir in flour, salt and pepper. Cook over medium heat, stirring constantly, until smooth and bubbly; remove from heat. Stir in milk. Heat to boiling, stirring constantly. Boil and stir 1 minute. Gradually stir at least half of the hot mixture into egg; stir back into hot mixture in saucepan. Boil and stir 1 minute; remove from heat. Stir in cheese.

NUTRITION PER SERVING: Calories 615; Protein 33g; Carbohydrate 30g (Dietary Fiber 6g); Fat 43g (Unsaturated 29g, Saturated 14g); Cholesterol 190mg; Sodium 1110mg.

PERCENT OF U.S. RDA: Vitamin A 32%; Vitamin C 8%; Calcium 30%; Iron 16%

Spiced Orange Ribs

1 to 1½ pounds pork country-style ribs or ¾ pound pork boneless country-style ribs

1 teaspoon ground ginger

1 teaspoon ground cinnamon

1 teaspoon ground paprika

½ teaspoon salt

¼ teaspoon pepper

⅓ cup orange marmalade

3 tablespoons orange juice

1 teaspoon Dijon mustard or other prepared mustard

Cut pork ribs into serving pieces if necessary. Place pork, meaty sides up, in single layer in ungreased shallow pan. Mix ginger, cinnamon, paprika, salt and pepper; rub onto meaty sides of pork. Cover with plastic wrap and refrigerate at least 4 hours.

Heat oven to 325°. Heat marmalade, orange juice and mustard in 1-quart saucepan over medium heat, stirring occasionally, until marmalade is melted. Pour orange sauce over pork. Cover with aluminum foil and bake about 45 minutes, spooning sauce over pork occasionally, until pork is almost tender. Uncover and bake 15 minutes longer or until pork is tender and no longer pink in center. Serve sauce over pork. *2 servings.*

NUTRITION PER SERVING: Calories 465; Protein 19g; Carbohydrate 39g (Dietary Fiber 2g); Fat 27g (Unsaturated 17g, Saturated 10g); Cholesterol 80mg; Sodium 640mg.

PERCENT OF U.S. RDA: Vitamin A 6%; Vitamin C 12%; Calcium 4%; Iron 12%

SUPER SALADS

Tired of the same old green salad? You'll find that it's easy to prepare terrific salads for two. These delicious recipes will add color and variety to your meals. For a quick meal, serve them with main dish soups or sandwiches. Try these recipes for a tasty new twist!

Hurry-Up Potato Salad

(Photograph on page 92)

2 cups frozen hash brown potatoes with onions and peppers
¼ cup shredded carrot
¼ cup sour cream
2 tablespoons mayonnaise or salad dressing
¼ teaspoon curry powder
⅛ teaspoon salt
⅛ teaspoon ground mustard

Heat 1 inch water (salted if desired) to boiling in 1-quart saucepan. Add potatoes. Cover and heat to boiling; reduce heat. Simmer 6 to 8 minutes or until potatoes are tender; drain.

Mix remaining ingredients in medium glass or plastic bowl. Fold in potatoes. Cover and refrigerate at least 1 hour. *2 servings.*

NUTRITION PER SERVING: Calories 455; Protein 3g; Carbohydrate 33g (Dietary Fiber 3g); Fat 36g (Unsaturated 26g, Saturated 10g); Cholesterol 30mg; Sodium 630mg.

PERCENT OF U.S. RDA: Vitamin A 26%; Vitamin C 10%; Calcium 4%; Iron 4%

Orange Salad with Blackberry Dressing

(Photograph on page 39)

It's easy to turn this salad into a main dish— just add salad greens and sliced grilled chicken breast halves.

2 small oranges, sliced
4 thin slices onion, separated into rings
2 tablespoons slivered almonds, toasted (see page 8)
½ cup fresh or frozen (slightly thawed) blackberries
2 tablespoons almond or vegetable oil
1 tablespoon raspberry or white vinegar
1 tablespoon water
½ teaspoon sugar
⅛ teaspoon ground nutmeg

Arrange orange slices on 2 salad plates. Top with onion rings and sprinkle with almonds.

Place remaining ingredients in blender. Cover and blend until smooth. Serve dressing with salads. *2 servings.*

NUTRITION PER SERVING: Calories 240; Protein 3g; Carbohydrate 21g (Dietary Fiber 4g); Fat 18g (Unsaturated 16g, Saturated 2g); Cholesterol 0mg; Sodium 5mg.

PERCENT OF U.S. RDA: Vitamin A 8%; Vitamin C 100%; Calcium 8%; Iron 4%

Fruity Coleslaw

(Photograph on page 86)

2 tablespoons vanilla or orange yogurt

1 tablespoon mayonnaise or salad dressing

1 cup chopped pear, apple or orange or 1 can (11 ounces) mandarin orange segments, drained

¾ cup coleslaw mix or shredded cabbage

2 tablespoons salted peanuts

Mix yogurt and mayonnaise. Toss remaining ingredients. Fold in yogurt mixture. *2 servings.*

NUTRITION PER SERVING: Calories 175; Protein 4g; Carbohydrate 19g (Dietary Fiber 4g); Fat 11g (Unsaturated 9g, Saturated 2g); Cholesterol 5mg; Sodium 90mg.

PERCENT OF U.S. RDA: Vitamin A *%; Vitamin C 20%; Calcium 4%; Iron 2%

Creamy Vegetable Salad

2 cups frozen mixed broccoli, cauliflower and carrots

¼ cup shredded Swiss cheese (1 ounce)

¼ cup ranch dressing

2 tablespoons sunflower nuts

1 tablespoon chopped fresh parsley

1 tablespoon milk

Cook frozen vegetables as directed on package; drain. Rinse with cold water; drain.

Mix vegetables and remaining ingredients in medium glass or plastic bowl. Cover and refrigerate at least 1 hour. *2 servings.*

NUTRITION PER SERVING: Calories 260; Protein 10g; Carbohydrate 14g (Dietary Fiber 4g); Fat 20g (Unsaturated 15g, Saturated 5g); Cholesterol 25mg; Sodium 350mg.

PERCENT OF U.S. RDA: Vitamin A 100%; Vitamin C 40%; Calcium 22%; Iron 8%

Zucchini-Couscous Salad

(Photograph on page 95)

½ cup chicken broth

¼ cup uncooked couscous

½ cup shredded zucchini

¼ cup chopped green, red or yellow bell pepper

2 tablespoons white vinegar or white wine vinegar

1 tablespoon vegetable oil

1 teaspoon chopped fresh or ¼ teaspoon dried savory leaves

1 teaspoon sesame oil

½ teaspoon sugar

Lettuce leaves, if desired

Heat broth to boiling in 1-quart saucepan; remove from heat. Stir in couscous. Cover and let stand 5 minutes.

Mix couscous, zucchini and bell pepper in medium glass or plastic bowl. Shake remaining ingredients in tightly covered container. Pour over couscous mixture; stir to coat. Cover and refrigerate at least 1 hour. Serve on lettuce leaves. *2 servings.*

NUTRITION PER SERVING: Calories 190; Protein 4g; Carbohydrate 22g (Dietary Fiber 1g); Fat 10g (Unsaturated 8g, Saturated 2g); Cholesterol 0mg; Sodium 200mg.

PERCENT OF U.S. RDA: Vitamin A 2%; Vitamin C 20%; Calcium 2%; Iron 4%

Jambalaya

This classic one-pot dish from Cajun country in Louisiana is pronounced "jam-ba-LIE-ya." Its name comes from *jambon,* **the French word for "ham."**

4 pork sausage links, cut into bite-size pieces

½ cup uncooked regular long grain rice

¼ cup sliced celery

¼ cup chopped green bell pepper

1 small onion, chopped (about ¼ cup)

2 cloves garlic, finely chopped

1 can (8 ounces) stewed tomatoes

1 can (8 ounces) tomato sauce

½ cup water

1½ teaspoons chopped fresh or ½ teaspoon dried thyme leaves

⅛ to ¼ teaspoon ground red pepper (cayenne)

⅛ teaspoon salt

1 bay leaf

½ cup diced fully cooked smoked ham

Chopped fresh parsley, if desired

Cook sausage in 1½-quart saucepan over medium heat, stirring frequently, until brown. Remove sausage and reserve. Drain fat from saucepan, reserving 2 tablespoons in saucepan. Cook rice, celery, bell pepper, onion and garlic in fat in saucepan over medium-high heat about 6 minutes, stirring frequently, until rice is light brown.

Stir in tomatoes, tomato sauce, water, thyme, red pepper, salt and bay leaf. Heat to boiling; reduce heat to low. Cover and simmer about 20 minutes, stirring frequently, just until rice is tender. Stir in sausage and ham. Cover and simmer just until ham is hot. Remove bay leaf. Sprinkle with parsley. *2 servings.*

NUTRITION PER SERVING: Calories 380; Protein 19g; Carbohydrate 55g (Dietary Fiber 4g); Fat 11g (Unsaturated 7g, Saturated 4g); Cholesterol 40mg; Sodium 1790mg.

PERCENT OF U.S. RDA: Vitamin A 20%; Vitamin C 44%; Calcium 8%; Iron 24%

Fettuccine with Ham and Goat Cheese

(Photograph on page 44)

8 ounces uncooked fresh refrigerated or 4 ounces uncooked dried fettuccine or spinach fettuccine

¾ cup diced fully cooked smoked ham

½ cup sour cream

½ cup milk

1 tablespoon margarine or butter

2 medium green onions, thinly sliced

¼ cup sliced pitted ripe olives

¼ cup crumbled goat cheese (such as Montrachet) or feta cheese (1 ounce)

1 tablespoon chopped fresh parsley

Freshly ground pepper

Cook fettuccine as directed on package; drain and keep warm. Heat ham, sour cream, milk, margarine and onions in 1-quart saucepan over low heat, stirring constantly, just until hot. Stir in olives. Toss with fettuccine. Sprinkle with cheese, parsley and pepper. *2 servings.*

NUTRITION PER SERVING: Calories 515; Protein 24g; Carbohydrate 45g (Dietary Fiber 3g); Fat 28g (Unsaturated 15g, Saturated 13g); Cholesterol 130mg; Sodium 1310mg.

PERCENT OF U.S. RDA: Vitamin A 24%; Vitamin C 26%; Calcium 4%; Iron 12%

Warm Black Bean and Sausage Salad

The spices in chorizo sausage make it reddish in color, so it can be difficult to tell when the sausage is fully cooked. Careful timing is the best way to know when the sausage is done.

Chile Dressing (below)

3 cups bite-size pieces mixed salad greens

½ cup frozen (thawed) whole kernel corn

½ cup diced jicama (about 3 ounces)

1 small tomato, seeded and chopped (about ½ cup)

1 green onion, sliced

1 uncooked chorizo or Italian sausage link (3 or 4 ounces), cut into ¼-inch slices

1 can (15 ounces) black beans, rinsed and drained

Prepare Chile Dressing. Mix remaining ingredients except sausage and black beans in large bowl. Cook sausage in 10-inch skillet over medium heat about 5 minutes, turning occasionally, until brown; drain. Stir in dressing and black beans; heat until hot. Pour over vegetable mixture; toss thoroughly. *2 servings.*

CHILE DRESSING

¼ cup red wine vinegar

1 tablespoon vegetable oil

¼ teaspoon chile powder

⅛ teaspoon ground cumin

1 small clove garlic, crushed

Mix all ingredients.

NUTRITION PER SERVING: Calories 765; Protein 42g; Carbohydrate 75g (Dietary Fiber 18g); Fat 41g (Unsaturated 27g, Saturated 14g); Cholesterol 75mg; Sodium 1580mg.

PERCENT OF U.S. RDA: Vitamin A 8%; Vitamin C 18%; Calcium 18%; Iron 44%

Spicy Italian Soup

Chervil, a mild-flavored member of the parsley family, has a slight taste of anise. Sprinkle additional chervil on each serving if desired.

½ pound hot or mild bulk Italian sausage

2 cloves garlic, finely chopped

¼ cup thinly sliced carrot

¼ cup uncooked elbow macaroni

2 cups beef broth

1 tablespoon chopped fresh or 1 teaspoon dried chervil or basil leaves

1 can (14 ounces) peeled Italian-style tomatoes, undrained

½ cup sliced zucchini

Grated Parmesan cheese, if desired

Cook sausage and garlic in 1½-quart saucepan, stirring occasionally, until sausage is brown; drain. Stir in remaining ingredients except zucchini; break up tomatoes. Heat to boiling; reduce heat. Stir in zucchini. Cover and simmer about 10 minutes, stirring occasionally, until macaroni and vegetables are tender. Serve with Parmesan cheese. *2 servings.*

NUTRITION PER SERVING: Calories 500; Protein 33g; Carbohydrate 28g (Dietary Fiber 4g); Fat 30g (Unsaturated 19g, Saturated 11g); Cholesterol 90mg; Sodium 2020mg.

PERCENT OF U.S. RDA: Vitamin A 36%; Vitamin C 32%; Calcium 12%; Iron 26%

Country Bratwurst Chowder

(Photograph on page 45)

1 can (14½ ounces) ready-to-serve chicken broth

1 large potato, peeled and cubed (about 1½ cups)

1 small onion, chopped (about ¼ cup)

1 tablespoon chopped fresh or 1 teaspoon dried oregano leaves

¼ teaspoon pepper

1 cup fresh or frozen (thawed and drained) broccoli cuts

¼ pound fully cooked smoked bratwurst or smoked Polish sausage, sliced

1 cup half-and-half

½ cup shredded process Swiss cheese (2 ounces)

1 tablespoon chopped fresh or 1 teaspoon freeze-dried chives

Heat broth, potato, onion, oregano and pepper to boiling in 1½-quart saucepan; reduce heat. Cover and simmer 10 to 12 minutes, stirring occasionally, until potato is tender. Pour potato mixture into blender. Cover and blend on medium speed 15 seconds or until smooth. Pour back into saucepan. Stir in broccoli and bratwurst. Heat to boiling; reduce heat. Cover and simmer 5 minutes, stirring occasionally.

Stir in half-and-half. Cook over medium heat, stirring constantly, until hot. Sprinkle each serving with cheese and chives. *2 servings.*

NUTRITION PER SERVING: Calories 550; Protein 25g; Carbohydrate 27g (Dietary Fiber 3g); Fat 39g (Unsaturated 19g, Saturated 20g); Cholesterol 110mg; Sodium 1600mg.

PERCENT OF U.S. RDA: Vitamin A 20%; Vitamin C 36%; Calcium 40%; Iron 14%

Lemon-Tarragon Lamb Chops

2 lamb leg sirloin chops or 4 lamb rib chops (about 1 pound), 1 inch thick

½ lemon

1 tablespoon olive or vegetable oil

1 cup sliced mushrooms (about 3 ounces)

1 medium green onion, thinly sliced

1½ teaspoons chopped fresh or ½ teaspoon dried tarragon leaves

1 teaspoon lemon juice

½ teaspoon lemon pepper

3 tablespoons dry white wine or chicken broth

⅓ cup whipping (heavy) cream

Cut outer edge of fat on lamb chops diagonally at 1-inch intervals to prevent curling (do not cut into meat). Squeeze juice from ½ lemon over both sides of lamb. Heat oil in 10-inch skillet over medium heat until hot. Cook lamb in oil 10 to 12 minutes for medium (160°), turning once. Remove lamb; keep warm. Drain fat from skillet, reserving 1 tablespoon in skillet.

Cook mushrooms, onion, tarragon, 1 teaspoon lemon juice and the lemon pepper in oil over medium-high heat 4 minutes, stirring occasionally. Stir in wine. Cook about 3 minutes, stirring occasionally, until liquid is reduced by half. Stir in whipping cream. Heat to boiling. Boil gently 1 minute. Serve mushroom mixture over lamb. *2 servings.*

NUTRITION PER SERVING: Calories 340; Protein 24g; Carbohydrate 4g (Dietary Fiber 1g); Fat 26g (Unsaturated 14g, Saturated 12g); Cholesterol 115mg; Sodium 75mg.

PERCENT OF U.S. RDA: Vitamin A 10%; Vitamin C 2%; Calcium 4%; Iron 14%

Lamb Chops with Fruited Rice

(*Photograph on page 46*)

In a pinch, you can substitute raisins for the dried fruit mixture.

2 lamb shoulder blade chops (about ¾ pound), 1 inch thick

1 teaspoon olive or vegetable oil

1½ cups beef broth

½ cup uncooked regular long grain rice

⅓ cup diced dried fruit and raisin mixture

1 small onion, chopped (about ¼ cup)

1 teaspoon curry powder

¼ cup chopped walnuts

1 tablespoon chopped fresh parsley

Cut outer edge of fat on lamb chops diagonally at 1-inch intervals to prevent curling (do not cut into meat). Cook lamb in oil in 10-inch skillet over medium heat about 5 minutes, turning once, until brown on both sides. Remove lamb; keep warm. Drain fat from skillet.

Mix broth, rice, dried fruit, onion and curry powder in same skillet. Place lamb on top. Heat to boiling; reduce heat. Cover and simmer about 20 minutes or until rice and lamb are tender. (Do not lift cover or stir.) Remove lamb; keep warm. Stir walnuts and parsley into rice mixture. Serve with lamb. *2 servings.*

NUTRITION PER SERVING: Calories 550; Protein 36g; Carbohydrate 58g (Dietary Fiber 4g); Fat 21g (Unsaturated 16g, Saturated 5g); Cholesterol 85mg; Sodium 560mg.

PERCENT OF U.S. RDA: Vitamin A 6%; Vitamin C 4%; Calcium 6%; Iron 28%

Lamb and Vegetable Skillet

½ pound ground lamb

2 tablespoons chopped onion

1 clove garlic, finely chopped

1 tablespoon lemon juice

2 teaspoons chopped fresh or ¾ teaspoon dried rosemary leaves

¼ teaspoon pepper

½ package (16-ounce size) frozen mixed broccoli, carrots and water chestnuts, thawed and well drained (about 2 cups)

¼ cup shredded Swiss cheese (1 ounce)

Mix ground lamb, onion, garlic, lemon juice, 1 teaspoon of the rosemary and ⅛ teaspoon of the pepper. Shape mixture into 2 patties, each about ½ inch thick. Cook patties in 10-inch skillet over medium heat without turning about 10 minutes or until well browned. Drain fat from skillet; turn patties.

Place vegetables on lamb. Sprinkle with remaining rosemary and pepper. Cover and cook over medium heat about 8 minutes or until lamb patties are no longer pink in center and vegetables are tender. Sprinkle with cheese. *2 servings.*

NUTRITION PER SERVING: Calories 300; Protein 25g; Carbohydrate 8g (Dietary Fiber 3g); Fat 20g (Unsaturated 10g, Saturated 10g); Cholesterol 85mg; Sodium 120mg.

PERCENT OF U.S. RDA: Vitamin A 22%; Vitamin C 38%; Calcium 20%; Iron 12%

CHAPTER

③

▚▚▚▚▚▚▚ MENUS ▚▚▚▚▚▚▚

SPECIAL OCCASION DINNER

Champagne

Brie cheese with crackers

Dilled Fettuccine with Whiskey-Crab Sauce
(page 60)

Romaine lettuce with raspberry vinaigrette

Popovers

Broiled brown sugar–topped pineapple
slices

✖

ART GALLERY CRAWL

Mushroom Manicotti (page 63)

Mixed greens with Italian dressing

Garlic bread

Ice cream • Biscotti

✖

PRE-THEATER DINNER

Spinach-stuffed Pinwheels (page 62)

Steamed carrots

Marinated vegetable salad

Chocolate truffles • Flavored coffee

✖

VIDEO MARATHON

Hot and Spicy Chile (page 73)

Pickles and relishes

Tex-Mex Corn Muffins (page 67)

Ice cream bars

BEFORE THE GAME

Tomato-Tortellini Stew (page 65)

Assorted crudités

Rich Herbed Rye Biscuits (page 66)

Ice cream pie

✖

OFF TO THE MALL

Brown Rice and Cheese Casserole
(page 68)

Spinach salad

Sesame Fingers (page 67)

Cheesecake with fruit

✖

TOAST TO CINCO DE MAYO

Tortilla chips with guacamole or salsa

Mexican Bean Bake (page 71)

Sliced oranges and onions with sweet-and-
sour dressing

Soft flour tortillas

Cinnamon ice cream • Brownies

Margaritas or limeade

✖

SNOW DAY LUNCH

Hearty Bean and Pasta Stew (page 72)

Fruity Coleslaw (page 53)

Soft breadsticks

Butterscotch brownies

CHAPTER

3

PASTA, GRAINS AND LEGUMES

Four-Cheese Fettuccine

4 ounces uncooked spinach fettuccine

1 tablespoon margarine or butter

2 tablespoons sliced green onions

2 cloves garlic, finely chopped

⅓ cup half-and-half

¼ cup shredded provolone or Gouda cheese (1 ounce)

¼ cup crumbled blue or Stilton cheese (1 ounce)

¼ cup shredded Monterey Jack cheese (1 ounce)

2 tablespoons grated sapsago or Parmesan cheese

2 tablespoons pistachio nuts or toasted pecans (page 8), coarsely chopped

Cook fettuccine as directed on package; drain. While fettuccine is cooking, heat margarine in 1½-quart saucepan over medium heat until melted. Cook onions and garlic in margarine about 3 minutes, stirring frequently, until onions are softened; reduce heat to low. Stir in half-and-half and cheeses. Heat, stirring occasionally, just until cheese is melted. Stir fettuccine into cheese mixture; heat until hot. Sprinkle each serving with nuts. *2 servings.*

NUTRITION PER SERVING: Calories 525; Protein 23g; Carbohydrate 43g (Dietary Fiber 4g); Fat 31g (Unsaturated 17g, Saturated 14g); Cholesterol 105mg; Sodium 880mg.

PERCENT OF U.S. RDA: Vitamin A 24%; Vitamin C *%; Calcium 44%; Iron 18%

Dilled Fettuccine with Whiskey-Crab Sauce

(Photograph on page 47)

4 ounces uncooked fettuccine

1 tablespoon olive or vegetable oil

1 jar (6 ounces) marinated artichoke hearts, drained

1 tablespoon margarine or butter

2 tablespoons sliced green onions

½ cup Scotch whiskey, bourbon or chicken broth

1½ teaspoons chopped fresh or ½ teaspoon dried dill weed

⅛ teaspoon salt

⅛ teaspoon pepper

¾ cup whipping (heavy) cream

1 cup cut-up cooked crabmeat or frozen (thawed) salad-style imitation crabmeat or 1 can (6 ounces) crabmeat, drained and cartilage removed

¼ cup slivered almonds, toasted (page 8)

1 green onion, cut diagonally into thin slices

Cook fettuccine as directed on package; drain. Toss fettuccine and oil; keep warm. Cut artichoke hearts into halves if necessary. Heat margarine in 10-inch skillet over medium heat until melted. Cook 2 tablespoons onions in margarine about 3 minutes, stirring frequently, until tender. Stir in whiskey, dill weed, salt and pepper. Cook over medium-high heat about 3 minutes, stirring occasionally, until almost all liquid has evaporated.

Stir whipping cream into whiskey mixture. Heat to boiling, stirring constantly. Cook over medium-high heat about 3 minutes, stirring frequently, until slightly thickened. Stir in artichoke hearts and crabmeat; heat through. Toss sauce and fettuccine. Sprinkle with slivered almonds and onion. *2 servings.*

NUTRITION PER SERVING: Calories 815; Protein 28g; Carbohydrate 51g (Dietary Fiber 6g); Fat 58g (Unsaturated 34g, Saturated 24g); Cholesterol 240mg; Sodium 860mg.

PERCENT OF U.S. RDA: Vitamin A 38%; Vitamin C 10%; Calcium 22%; Iron 26%

Linguine alla Carbonara

4 ounces uncooked linguine or fettuccine

1 tablespoon margarine or butter

4 slices bacon, cut into 1-inch pieces

½ cup thinly sliced leek

2 eggs, beaten

½ cup half-and-half

⅛ teaspoon ground nutmeg

⅛ teaspoon freshly ground pepper

¼ cup grated Romano or Parmesan cheese

¼ cup shredded Swiss cheese (1 ounce)

Cook linguine as directed on package; drain. Toss linguine and margarine. Cook bacon in 10-inch skillet over medium heat, stirring occasionally, until crisp. Remove bacon from skillet with slotted spoon; drain. Reserve 1 tablespoon bacon fat in skillet.

Cook leek in bacon fat over medium heat about 3 minutes, stirring occasionally, until tender. Stir in eggs, half-and-half, nutmeg and pepper. Cook over medium-low heat about 3 minutes, stirring constantly, until warm. Toss egg mixture and linguine. Toss linguine mixture, bacon and cheeses. *2 servings.*

NUTRITION PER SERVING: Calories 595; Protein 28g; Carbohydrate 51g (Dietary Fiber 2g); Fat 32g (Unsaturated 18g, Saturated 14g); Cholesterol 270mg; Sodium 810mg.

PERCENT OF U.S. RDA: Vitamin A 36%; Vitamin C 10%; Calcium 38%; Iron 18%

Sweet-'n'-Sour Pasta

*4 ounces uncooked spaghetti or linguine,
   broken into 3-inch pieces*

⅓ cup apple juice

2 tablespoons packed brown sugar

1 tablespoon rice vinegar or white vinegar

1 tablespoon soy sauce

1½ teaspoons cornstarch

½ teaspoon ground ginger

½ pound firm tofu, cut into ¾-inch cubes

1 tablespoon vegetable oil

*1 medium carrot, thinly sliced (about ½
   cup)*

*3 medium stalks bok choy (with leaves),
   cut diagonally into ½-inch slices*

1 tablespoon vegetable oil

⅓ cup coarsely chopped peanuts

Cook spaghetti as directed on package; drain. Rinse in cold water; drain. Mix apple juice, brown sugar, vinegar, soy sauce, cornstarch and ginger; reserve. Drain tofu cubes thoroughly.

Heat wok or 10-inch skillet over high heat until 1 or 2 drops of water bubble and skitter when sprinkled in wok. Add 1 tablespoon oil; rotate wok to coat side. Add carrot; stir-fry 2 minutes. Add bok choy; stir-fry about 3 minutes or until vegetables are crisp-tender. Remove vegetable mixture from wok.

Add 1 tablespoon oil to wok; rotate to coat side. Add tofu; gently stir-fry 5 minutes. Stir in apple juice mixture. Cook and stir about 1 minute or until thickened. Stir in spaghetti and vegetable mixture; heat through. Sprinkle with peanuts. *2 servings.*

NUTRITION PER SERVING: Calories 775; Protein 34g; Carbohydrate 82g (Dietary Fiber 8g); Fat 38g (Unsaturated 33g, Saturated 5g); Cholesterol 0mg; Sodium 800mg.

PERCENT OF U.S. RDA: Vitamin A 100%; Vitamin C 14%; Calcium 36%; Iron 90%

Basil-Tomato Pasta

*4 ounces uncooked linguine, fettuccine or
   spaghetti*

Basil-Tomato Sauce (below)

¼ cup sour cream

2 tablespoons grated Parmesan cheese

Cook linguine as directed on package; drain. While linguine is cooking, prepare Basil-Tomato Sauce. Serve sauce over linguine. Top with sour cream. Sprinkle with cheese. *2 servings.*

BASIL-TOMATO SAUCE

1 tablespoon olive or vegetable oil

½ cup thinly sliced leek

2 cloves garlic, finely chopped

*1 tablespoon chopped fresh or 1 teaspoon
   dried basil leaves*

*2 tablespoons dry white wine or chicken
   broth*

⅛ teaspoon salt

*1 ounce thinly sliced pepperoni, cut into
   ¼-inch strips (about ¼ cup)*

1 can (8 ounces) stewed tomatoes

*1 jar (2½ ounces) sliced mushrooms,
   drained*

Heat oil in 1½-quart saucepan over medium heat until hot. Cook leek and garlic in oil about 3 minutes, stirring frequently, until leek is tender. Stir in remaining ingredients. Heat to boiling.

NUTRITION PER SERVING: Calories 520; Protein 17g; Carbohydrate 64g (Dietary Fiber 5g); Fat 24g (Unsaturated 16g, Saturated 8g); Cholesterol 35mg; Sodium 1170mg.

PERCENT OF U.S. RDA: Vitamin A 28%; Vitamin C 20%; Calcium 16%; Iron 22%

Spinach-stuffed Pinwheels

(Photograph on page 81)

2 uncooked lasagne noodles

1 package (10 ounces) frozen chopped spinach

½ cup small curd creamed cottage cheese

1 tablespoon chopped fresh or 1 teaspoon dried oregano leaves

¼ teaspoon garlic powder

1 tablespoon margarine or butter

1 tablespoon all-purpose flour

¼ teaspoon salt

⅛ teaspoon ground nutmeg

1 cup milk

½ cup shredded Swiss cheese (2 ounces)

½ cup shredded mozzarella cheese (2 ounces)

Grated Parmesan cheese, if desired

Cook noodles as directed on package; drain. Rinse in cold water; drain. Cut noodles lengthwise into halves. While noodles are cooking, cook spinach as directed on package; drain thoroughly. Press spinach between several layers of paper towels to squeeze out excess liquid. Mix spinach, cottage cheese, oregano and garlic powder.

Heat oven to 350°. Grease 2 individual gratin dishes or oval 16-ounce casseroles. Heat margarine in 1½-quart saucepan over medium heat until melted. Stir in flour, salt and nutmeg. Cook over medium heat, stirring constantly, until mixture is smooth and bubbly; remove from heat. Stir in milk. Heat to boiling, stirring constantly. Boil and stir 1 minute; reduce heat. Stir in Swiss and mozzarella cheeses until melted.

Loosely roll up each noodle strip. Arrange 2 noodle rolls, cut side down, in each dish. Spread each noodle roll gently apart, using fingers, until 2½ inches in diameter, making space in center for spinach filling. Spoon spinach filling into noodle rolls. Pour cheese sauce over noodle rolls. Sprinkle with Parmesan cheese. Cover with aluminum foil and bake about 20 minutes or until hot and bubbly. *2 servings.*

NUTRITION PER SERVING: Calories 465; Protein 32g; Carbohydrate 34g (Dietary Fiber 2g); Fat 23g (Unsaturated 11g, Saturated 12g); Cholesterol 55mg; Sodium 990mg.

PERCENT OF U.S. RDA: Vitamin A 98%; Vitamin C 10%; Calcium 80%; Iron 16%

Creamy Zucchini Lasagne

There's no better accompaniment to this wonderful lasagne than crusty, golden slices of garlic bread.

2 uncooked lasagne noodles

1 tablespoon margarine or butter

1 medium zucchini, cut into julienne strips

2 tablespoons sliced green onions

2 cloves garlic, finely chopped

1 egg, beaten

½ cup ricotta or small curd creamed cottage cheese, drained

2 tablespoons grated Parmesan cheese

1 tablespoon chopped fresh or 1 teaspoon dried marjoram leaves

1 cup spaghetti sauce

1 cup shredded mozzarella cheese (4 ounces)

2 tablespoons grated Parmesan cheese

Heat oven to 350°. Cook noodles as directed on package; drain. Rinse in cold water; drain. Cut noodles crosswise into halves. Heat margarine in 10-inch skillet over medium heat until melted. Cook zucchini, onions and garlic in margarine about 3 minutes, stirring frequently, until zucchini is crisp-tender; drain. Mix egg, ricotta cheese, 2 tablespoons Parmesan cheese and the marjoram.

Spread ¼ cup of the spaghetti sauce in each of 2 ungreased individual 16-ounce casseroles or au gratin dishes. Top each with 1 noodle half. Spread one-fourth of the ricotta mixture over each noodle half. Top each with one-fourth of the zucchini mixture. Sprinkle each with one-fourth of the mozzarella cheese. Continue layering with remaining noodles, ricotta mixture, spaghetti sauce and zucchini mixture. Sprinkle with remaining mozzarella cheese and 2 tablespoons Parmesan cheese.

Cover with aluminum foil and bake 20 minutes. Uncover and bake about 10 minutes longer or until hot and bubbly. Let stand 10 minutes before serving. *2 servings.*

NUTRITION PER SERVING: Calories 550; Protein 35g; Carbohydrate 39g (Dietary Fiber 6g); Fat 31g (Unsaturated 17g, Saturated 14g); Cholesterol 160mg; Sodium 1560mg.

PERCENT OF U.S. RDA: Vitamin A 38%; Vitamin C 10%; Calcium 84%; Iron 22%

Mushroom Manicotti

(*Photograph on page 48*)

Blue cheese and farmer's cheese are also delicious in the filling.

4 uncooked manicotti shells

Garlic-Mushroom Sauce (right)

1 package (3 ounces) cream cheese, softened

3 tablespoons crumbled feta cheese

2 tablespoons chopped onion

½ teaspoon Worcestershire sauce

¼ cup diced fully cooked smoked ham

1 tablespoon chopped fresh or 1 teaspoon freeze-dried chives

Heat oven to 350°. Cook manicotti shells as directed on package; drain. Prepare Garlic-Mushroom Sauce in same saucepan.

Mix cream cheese, feta cheese, onion and Worcestershire sauce in small bowl, using fork, until well blended. Stir in ham and chives. Fill each shell with about 3 tablespoons of the cheese mixture, using small spoon.

Pour half of the sauce into ungreased square baking dish, 8×8×2 inches. Arrange filled shells in baking dish. Spoon remaining sauce over shells. Cover with aluminum foil and bake about 20 minutes or until hot and bubbly. *2 servings.*

GARLIC-MUSHROOM SAUCE

1 tablespoon margarine or butter

2 cups sliced mushrooms (about 5 ounces)

2 tablespoons chopped onion

2 cloves garlic, finely chopped

⅓ cup dry sherry, dry white wine or chicken broth

1 teaspoon lemon juice

¼ teaspoon lemon pepper

⅛ teaspoon salt

½ cup whipping (heavy) cream

Heat margarine in 3-quart saucepan over medium heat until melted. Cook mushrooms, onion and garlic in margarine about 3 minutes, stirring frequently, until vegetables are crisp-tender. Stir in sherry, lemon juice, lemon pepper and salt. Cook over medium-high heat about 4 minutes, stirring occasionally, until almost all liquid has evaporated. Stir in whipping cream. Heat to boiling, stirring constantly. Boil over medium-high heat about 1 minute, stirring frequently, until slightly thickened.

NUTRITION PER SERVING: Calories 605; Protein 14g; Carbohydrate 31g (Dietary Fiber 2g); Fat 48g (Unsaturated 21g, Saturated 27g); Cholesterol 150mg; Sodium 730mg.

PERCENT OF U.S. RDA: Vitamin A 42%; Vitamin C 6%; Calcium 14%; Iron 16%

Ravioli-Vegetable Soup

2 cups frozen mixed cauliflower, carrots, broccoli and lima beans

4 ounces uncooked refrigerated or frozen (thawed) meat- or cheese-filled ravioli (about ⅔ cup)

¼ cup bite-size pieces smoked cooked turkey or chicken

3 cups chicken broth

1 tablespoon chopped fresh or 1 teaspoon dried basil leaves

1½ teaspoons chopped fresh or ½ teaspoon dried rosemary leaves

⅛ teaspoon pepper

Grated Parmesan cheese

Mix all ingredients except cheese in 1½-quart saucepan. Heat to boiling; reduce heat. Cover and simmer 12 to 15 minutes, stirring occasionally, until vegetables are tender. Sprinkle each serving with cheese. *2 servings.*

NUTRITION PER SERVING: Calories 280; Protein 25g; Carbohydrate 25g (Dietary Fiber 5g); Fat 11g (Unsaturated 7g, Saturated 4g); Cholesterol 100mg; Sodium 1410mg.

PERCENT OF U.S. RDA: Vitamin A 100%; Vitamin C 40%; Calcium 26%; Iron 18%

Tex-Mex Tortellini Salad

If you prefer a milder salad, use Monterey Jack instead of the hot pepper cheese.

4 ounces dried cheese-filled tortellini (about 1 cup)

1 tablespoon olive or vegetable oil

¼ cup white vinegar

2 tablespoons chopped drained oil-packed sun-dried tomatoes

2 tablespoons water

1 tablespoon chopped fresh or 1 teaspoon dried basil leaves

¼ teaspoon ground mustard or 1 teaspoon Dijon mustard

1 medium avocado, peeled and cubed

¾ cup shredded hot pepper cheese (3 ounces)

Spinach leaves

Cook tortellini as directed on package; drain. Rinse in cold water; drain. Toss tortellini and oil in medium glass or plastic bowl. Shake vinegar, tomatoes, water, basil and mustard in tightly covered container; stir into tortellini. Cover and refrigerate at least 2 hours or until chilled. Just before serving, toss with avocado and cheese. Serve on spinach leaves. *2 servings.*

NUTRITION PER SERVING: Calories 480; Protein 19g; Carbohydrate 21g (Dietary Fiber 5g); Fat 38g (Unsaturated 25g, Saturated 13g); Cholesterol 110mg; Sodium 520mg.

PERCENT OF U.S. RDA: Vitamin A 34%; Vitamin C 10%; Calcium 40%; Iron 16%

Tomato-Tortellini Stew

2 slices bacon, cut into 1-inch pieces

1 medium stalk celery, sliced (about ½ cup)

1 small onion, chopped (about ¼ cup)

2 cloves garlic, finely chopped

2 cups beef broth

1 teaspoon chile powder

½ teaspoon sugar

⅛ teaspoon pepper

1 can (5½ ounces) spicy or regular eight-vegetable juice

4 ounces dried cheese-filled tortellini (about 1 cup)

½ cup shredded Cheddar cheese (2 ounces)

Cook bacon in 1½-quart saucepan over medium heat, stirring occasionally, until crisp. Remove bacon from saucepan with slotted spoon; drain. Reserve 1 tablespoon bacon fat in saucepan. Cook celery, onion and garlic in bacon fat about 3 minutes, stirring frequently, until vegetables are tender.

Stir in remaining ingredients except cheese. Heat to boiling; reduce heat. Cover and simmer about 15 minutes, stirring occasionally, until tortellini are tender. Sprinkle each serving with bacon and cheese. *2 servings.*

NUTRITION PER SERVING: Calories 355; Protein 24g; Carbohydrate 26g (Dietary Fiber 3g); Fat 20g (Unsaturated 10g, Saturated 10g); Cholesterol 120mg; Sodium 1410mg.

PERCENT OF U.S. RDA: Vitamin A 26%; Vitamin C 20%; Calcium 34%; Iron 14%

Rigatoni and Fruit Salad

For a lovely light summer supper, serve this main dish salad with oat bran muffins and a scoop of raspberry sherbet for dessert.

4 ounces uncooked rigatoni or ziti (about 1 cup)

1 tablespoon olive or vegetable oil

1 orange, peeled and sectioned

1 can (8 ounces) pineapple chunks in juice, drained and 2 tablespoons juice reserved

½ cup diced fully cooked smoked ham

2 ounces Colby or Swiss cheese, cut into julienne strips

½ cup sour cream or plain yogurt

⅛ teaspoon ground cinnamon

¼ cup cashew pieces

Leaf lettuce

Chopped chives, if desired

Cook rigatoni as directed on package; drain. Rinse in cold water; drain. Toss rigatoni and oil in medium glass or plastic bowl. Mix in orange sections, pineapple chunks, ham and cheese. Mix reserved pineapple juice, the sour cream and cinnamon; stir into rigatoni mixture. Cover and refrigerate at least 2 hours or until chilled. Stir in cashews. Serve on lettuce. Sprinkle with chives. *2 servings.*

NUTRITION PER SERVING: Calories 750; Protein 27g; Carbohydrate 70g (Dietary Fiber 7g); Fat 43g (Unsaturated 25g, Saturated 18g); Cholesterol 140mg; Sodium 890mg.

PERCENT OF U.S. RDA: Vitamin A 20%; Vitamin C 50%; Calcium 28%; Iron 24%

QUICK AND EASY BREADS

Have you always shied away from making special breads because the batches are just too big? Here are 6 terrific recipes just for two, with few (if any) leftovers. These recipes take surprisingly little time to prepare, so you can even make biscuits in about 15 minutes from start to finish. What a great way to make lunch or dinner more special!

Cheesy Garlic Biscuits

(Photograph on page 43)

1 cup Bisquick® Original baking mix
⅓ cup milk
¼ cup shredded Cheddar cheese (1 ounce)
2 tablespoons margarine or butter, melted
⅛ teaspoon garlic powder

Heat oven to 450°. Mix baking mix, milk and cheese until soft dough forms; beat vigorously 30 seconds. Drop dough by 5 or 6 spoonfuls onto ungreased cookie sheet. Bake 8 to 10 minutes or until golden brown. Mix margarine and garlic powder; brush over warm biscuits before removing from cookie sheet. Serve warm. *5 or 6 biscuits.*

NUTRITION PER BISCUIT: Calories 160; Protein 3g; Carbohydrate 15g (Dietary Fiber 0g); Fat 10g (Unsaturated 7g, Saturated 3g); Cholesterol 10mg; Sodium 440mg.

PERCENT OF U.S. RDA: Vitamin A 8%; Vitamin C *%; Calcium 8%; Iron 4%

Rich Herbed Rye Biscuits

(Photograph on page 36)

2 tablespoons firm margarine or butter
⅓ cup all-purpose flour
¼ cup rye flour
1 tablespoon packed brown sugar
1 teaspoon baking powder
¼ teaspoon dried fines herbes
Dash of salt
1 egg white
1 tablespoon half-and-half or milk

Heat oven to 400°. Grease cookie sheet. Cut margarine into flours, brown sugar, baking powder, fines herbes and salt with pastry blender in medium bowl until mixture resembles fine crumbs. Stir in egg white and half-and-half.

Drop dough by 4 spoonfuls onto cookie sheet. Bake 12 to 14 minutes or until golden brown. Immediately remove from cookie sheet. Serve warm, or cool on wire rack. *4 biscuits.*

NUTRITION PER BISCUIT: Calories 125; Protein 2g; Carbohydrate 17g (Dietary Fiber 1g); Fat 6g (Unsaturated 5g, Saturated 1g); Cholesterol 5mg; Sodium 250mg.

PERCENT OF U.S. RDA: Vitamin A 8%; Vitamin C *%; Calcium 6%; Iron 4%

Orange-Pecan Muffins

(Photograph on page 87)

⅓ cup orange juice
2 tablespoons packed brown sugar
2 tablespoons margarine or butter, melted
1 egg white
¼ cup all-purpose flour
¼ cup whole wheat flour
1 teaspoon baking powder
¼ teaspoon grated orange peel
2 tablespoons finely chopped toasted pecans (page 8)

Heat oven to 400°. Grease bottoms only of 4 medium muffin cups, 2½×1¼ inches, or line with paper baking cups. Beat orange juice, brown

sugar, margarine and egg white in medium bowl. Stir in flours, baking powder and orange peel all at once just until flour is moistened (batter will be lumpy). Fold in pecans. Divide batter evenly among muffin cups. Bake 20 to 25 minutes or until golden brown. Immediately remove from pan. *4 muffins.*

NUTRITION PER MUFFIN: Calories 165; Protein 3g; Carbohydrate 21g (Dietary Fiber 1g); Fat 8g (Unsaturated 7g, Saturated 1g); Cholesterol 0mg; Sodium 180mg.

PERCENT OF U.S. RDA: Vitamin A 8%; Vitamin C 4%; Calcium 8%; Iron 4%

Tex-Mex Corn Muffins

(Photograph on page 84)

½ cup cornmeal

¼ cup all-purpose flour

⅓ cup milk

2 tablespoons vegetable oil

¾ teaspoon baking powder

⅛ teaspoon salt

1 egg

¼ cup shredded hot pepper cheese (1 ounce)

2 teaspoons chopped fresh parsley

Heat oven to 450°. Grease bottoms only of 4 medium muffin cups, 2½×1¼ inches. Mix all ingredients except cheese and parsley in medium bowl; beat vigorously 30 seconds. Fold in cheese and parsley. Divide batter evenly among muffin cups. Bake about 20 minutes or until golden. Immediately remove from pan. Serve warm. *4 muffins.*

NUTRITION PER MUFFIN: Calories 205; Protein 6g; Carbohydrate 21g (Dietary Fiber 1g); Fat 11g (Unsaturated 8g, Saturated 3g); Cholesterol 60mg; Sodium 210mg.

PERCENT OF U.S. RDA: Vitamin A 6%; Vitamin C *%; Calcium 12%; Iron 6%

Sesame Fingers

(Photograph on page 93)

2 tablespoons margarine or butter, softened

4 slices whole wheat bread

2 teaspoons sesame seed

Set oven control to broil. Spread margarine over bread. Sprinkle with sesame seed. Cut each slice into 4 strips. Place strips on rack in broiler pan. Broil 4 inches from heat 1½ to 2 minutes or until edges of bread are brown. *2 servings.*

NUTRITION PER SERVING: Calories 265; Protein 7g; Carbohydrate 28g (Dietary Fiber 3g); Fat 15g (Unsaturated 12g, Saturated 3g); Cholesterol 5mg; Sodium 440mg.

PERCENT OF U.S. RDA: Vitamin A 16%; Vitamin C *%; Calcium 6%; Iron 10%

Mediterranean Bread Crisps

(Photograph on page 85)

1 tablespoon margarine or butter, softened

1 tablespoon crumbled feta cheese

4 thin slices French bread

1 tablespoon chopped Greek or ripe olives

Heat oven to 400°. Mix margarine and cheese; spread over bread. Sprinkle with olives. Place on ungreased cookie sheet. Bake about 10 minutes or until crisp. *2 servings.*

NUTRITION PER SERVING: Calories 140; Protein 3g; Carbohydrate 17g (Dietary Fiber 1g); Fat 7g (Unsaturated 5g, Saturated 2g); Cholesterol 5mg; Sodium 380mg.

PERCENT OF U.S. RDA: Vitamin A 8%; Vitamin C *%; Calcium 4%; Iron 4%

Cheesy Polenta

Polenta is the Italian version of cornmeal mush that's frequently mixed with cheese, molded and then baked or fried. It's often topped with tomato sauce.

½ cup cornmeal

½ cup cold water

1½ cups boiling water

⅛ teaspoon salt

¾ cup shredded sharp Cheddar cheese (3 ounces)

1 tablespoon chopped fresh or 1 teaspoon freeze-dried chives

¼ cup grated Parmesan cheese

½ cup spaghetti sauce with meat

Grease two 10-ounce custard cups. Mix cornmeal and cold water in 1½-quart saucepan. Stir in boiling water and salt. Cook over medium heat, stirring constantly, until mixture thickens and boils; reduce heat to low. Cover and simmer 10 minutes, stirring occasionally; remove from heat. Stir in Cheddar cheese and chives until cheese is melted.

Spread one-fourth of the cornmeal mixture in each custard cup. Sprinkle each with 1 tablespoon of the Parmesan cheese. Repeat with remaining cornmeal mixture and Parmesan cheese. Cover and refrigerate at least 1 hour until firm and chilled through.

Heat oven to 350°. Cover the custard cups with aluminum foil and bake about 50 minutes or until hot in center. Meanwhile, heat spaghetti sauce in 1-quart saucepan until bubbly. Unmold polenta. Serve with spaghetti sauce. *2 servings.*

NUTRITION PER SERVING: Calories 370; Protein 18g; Carbohydrate 33g (Dietary Fiber 3g); Fat 20g (Unsaturated 9g, Saturated 11g); Cholesterol 50mg; Sodium 990mg.

PERCENT OF U.S. RDA: Vitamin A 16%; Vitamin C *%; Calcium 38%; Iron 12%

Brown Rice and Cheese Casserole

1½ cups water

½ cup uncooked regular brown rice

¼ teaspoon salt

¼ teaspoon ground mustard

⅛ teaspoon red pepper sauce

⅛ teaspoon pepper

1 small onion, chopped (about ¼ cup)

1 small green bell pepper, chopped (about ½ cup)

2 eggs

1 cup milk

½ cup shredded mozzarella cheese (2 ounces)

2 tablespoons grated Parmesan cheese

Heat water, rice, salt, mustard, pepper sauce and pepper to boiling in 2-quart saucepan, stirring once or twice; reduce heat. Cover and simmer 45 to 50 minutes or until rice is tender. Stir in onion and bell pepper.

Heat oven to 325°. Grease loaf dish, 9×5×3 inches. Spread rice mixture in loaf dish. Mix eggs and milk; pour over rice mixture. Sprinkle with cheeses.

Bake uncovered 25 to 30 minutes or until golden brown and set in center. Let stand 10 minutes. *2 servings.*

NUTRITION PER SERVING: Calories 395; Protein 25g; Carbohydrate 48g (Dietary Fiber 3g); Fat 13g (Unsaturated 7g, Saturated 6g); Cholesterol 230mg; Sodium 650mg.

PERCENT OF U.S. RDA: Vitamin A 20%; Vitamin C 10%; Calcium 48%; Iron 10%

Wheat Berry and Vegetable Soup

Wheat berries add a nutty flavor to this soup. If you can't find wheat berries in your supermarket, check a health food store.

3 cups beef broth

¾ cup uncooked wheat berries

¾ cup frozen whole kernel corn

½ cup frozen baby lima beans

¼ cup diced fully cooked smoked ham

1 tablespoon chopped fresh or 1 teaspoon dried marjoram leaves

1½ teaspoons chopped fresh or ¼ teaspoon dried thyme leaves

1 teaspoon Worcestershire sauce

⅛ teaspoon red pepper sauce

1 can (8 ounces) stewed tomatoes

Heat broth to boiling in 1½-quart saucepan. Stir in wheat berries. Cover and simmer 30 minutes, stirring occasionally. Stir in remaining ingredients. Heat to boiling; reduce heat. Cover and simmer about 12 minutes, stirring occasionally, until vegetables are tender. *2 servings.*

NUTRITION PER SERVING: Calories 465; Protein 25g; Carbohydrate 85g (Dietary Fiber 9g); Fat 7g (Unsaturated 5g, Saturated 2g); Cholesterol 10mg; Sodium 1470mg.

PERCENT OF U.S. RDA: Vitamin A 14%; Vitamin C 20%; Calcium 16%; Iron 30%

TAILORED FOR TWO
Great Grains

Rice is the most common of the grains on the market today and flavored rices make for nice variety. Stretch your culinary boundaries by trying other grains, such as bulgur, wheat berries, kasha or quinoa. Follow package directions for cooking method and amounts.

• General guidelines for cooking rice:

1. Heat rice, water and salt (if desired) to boiling in 1- to 1½-quart saucepan.

2. Reduce heat; cover and cook the specified amount of time. Fluff with fork and steam 5 to 10 minutes.

Type	Time in Minutes	Yield Per ½ cup Uncooked Rice
Regular	15	1½ cups
Parboiled (converted)	20 to 25	2 cups
Precooked (instant)	5	1 cup
Brown	50	2 cups
Wild rice	75 to 90	1½ cups

• Cooked rice can be stored tightly covered in the refrigerator up to five days or frozen in a covered container up to six months. To reheat, tightly cover and microwave on high about 1 minute per cup. Or place rice in heavy saucepan and add 2 tablespoons water per cup of cooked rice. Cover and cook over low heat about 5 minutes.

• The shorter the rice grain, the stickier the rice. Medium-grain rice works better than long grain rice in puddings because it is creamier.

Wild Rice–Vegetable Chowder

¼ cup uncooked wild rice

1¼ cups chicken broth

1 tablespoon margarine or butter

1 medium stalk celery, sliced (about ½ cup)

2 cloves garlic, finely chopped

½ cup frozen artichoke hearts (thawed)

¾ cup chicken broth

½ cup frozen small whole onions

1 tablespoon chopped fresh or 1 teaspoon dried thyme leaves

⅛ teaspoon pepper

1 cup shredded process Swiss cheese (4 ounces)

½ cup whipping (heavy) cream

Place wild rice in wire strainer. Run cold water through rice, lifting rice with fingers to clean thoroughly. Heat wild rice and 1¼ cups broth to boiling in 1-quart saucepan, stirring once or twice; reduce heat. Cover and simmer 45 to 50 minutes, stirring occasionally, until wild rice is tender. (Mixture will be watery; do not drain.)

Meanwhile, heat margarine in 1½-quart saucepan over medium heat until melted. Cook celery and garlic in margarine about 3 minutes, stirring frequently, until celery is softened. Cut up any large artichoke hearts.

Stir artichoke hearts, ¾ cup broth, the onions, thyme and pepper into celery mixture. Heat to boiling; reduce heat. Cover and simmer about 10 minutes, stirring occasionally, until vegetables are tender. Stir in wild rice mixture. Stir in cheese and whipping cream. Heat over low heat, stirring frequently, just until cheese is melted (do not boil). *2 servings.*

NUTRITION PER SERVING: Calories 630; Protein 26g; Carbohydrate 36g (Dietary Fiber 3g); Fat 44g (Unsaturated 19g, Saturated 25g); Cholesterol 130mg; Sodium 1030mg.

PERCENT OF U.S. RDA: Vitamin A 36%; Vitamin C 8%; Calcium 60%; Iron 12%

Herbed Lentils and Vegetables

(Photograph on page 83)

1½ cups chicken broth

¾ cup dried lentils, sorted and rinsed

1 small zucchini, sliced (about 1 cup)

1 small yellow squash, sliced (about 1 cup)

½ cup sliced green onions (about 5 medium)

1½ teaspoons chopped fresh or ½ teaspoon dried oregano leaves

¼ teaspoon ground thyme

2 large cloves garlic, finely chopped

1 jar (2 ounces) diced pimientos, drained

2 tablespoons grated Parmesan cheese

Heat broth and lentils to boiling in 2-quart nonstick saucepan, stirring occasionally. Cover and simmer 20 minutes. Stir in zucchini, squash, onions, oregano, thyme and garlic. Heat to boiling; reduce heat. Cover and simmer 5 minutes. Stir in pimientos. Simmer uncovered 2 to 3 minutes longer or until vegetables are crisp-tender and mixture is desired consistency. Sprinkle with cheese. *2 servings.*

NUTRITION PER SERVING: Calories 310; Protein 27g; Carbohydrate 55g (Dietary Fiber 14g); Fat 4g (Unsaturated 2g, Saturated 2g); Cholesterol 4mg; Sodium 690mg.

PERCENT OF U.S. RDA: Vitamin A 14%; Vitamin C 40%; Calcium 20%; Iron 52%

Cheese and Ham Tabbouleh Salad

(Photograph on page 82)

Serve this salad with Mediterranean Bread Crisps (page 67) and sliced fresh pears or apples.

½ cup uncooked bulgur

1 medium tomato, chopped (about ¾ cup)

½ cup chopped seeded cucumber

½ cup cubed Swiss cheese (2 ounces)

¼ cup diced fully cooked smoked ham

¼ cup chopped fresh parsley

2 tablespoons thinly sliced green onions

1 tablespoon chopped fresh or 1 teaspoon crushed dried mint leaves

3 tablespoons olive or vegetable oil

3 tablespoons lemon juice

⅛ teaspoon salt

⅛ teaspoon pepper

Lettuce leaves, if desired

Cover bulgur with cold water in bowl. Let stand 30 minutes; drain. Press out as much water as possible.

Place bulgur, tomato, cucumber, cheese, ham, parsley and onions in glass or plastic bowl. Mix remaining ingredients; pour over bulgur mixture and toss. Cover and refrigerate at least 4 hours or overnight. Serve bulgur mixture on lettuce leaves. *2 servings.*

NUTRITION PER SERVING: Calories 505; Protein 19g; Carbohydrate 49g (Dietary Fiber 11g); Fat 31g (Unsaturated 22g, Saturated 9g); Cholesterol 35mg; Sodium 400mg.

PERCENT OF U.S. RDA: Vitamin A 12%; Vitamin C 20%; Calcium 30%; Iron 16%

Mexican Bean Bake

½ cup Bisquick Original baking mix

2 tablespoons salsa

1 cup canned refried beans

2 tablespoons canned chopped green chiles, undrained

⅓ cup salsa

½ cup shredded Cheddar cheese (2 ounces)

½ cup shredded lettuce

¼ cup chopped tomato

2 tablespoons plain yogurt or sour cream

Heat oven to 375°. Grease loaf dish, 9×5×3 inches. Mix baking mix, 2 tablespoons salsa, the beans and chiles. Spread in loaf dish. Top with ⅓ cup salsa and the cheese. Bake uncovered 20 to 25 minutes or until set. Let stand 5 minutes. Top with lettuce, tomato and yogurt. *2 servings.*

NUTRITION PER SERVING: Calories 385; Protein 19g; Carbohydrate 50g (Dietary Fiber 7g); Fat 15g (Unsaturated 7g, Saturated 8g); Cholesterol 30mg; Sodium 1720mg.

PERCENT OF U.S. RDA: Vitamin A 20%; Vitamin C 26%; Calcium 30%; Iron 22%

TAILORED FOR TWO
Beans and Things

Dried beans, peas and lentils are part of the food category legumes. They are an excellent source of complex carbohydrates.

• When cooking for two, it is often most efficient to use canned or frozen beans.

• Try the new varieties of beans with added spices to spark up your favorite dishes.

• Lentils cook relatively quickly (about 20 minutes) and are suitable for small amounts.

• Dishes containing beans freeze quite well. However, the skin of some beans may break.

Hearty Bean and Pasta Stew

½ cup uncooked shell macaroni

2 tablespoons chopped green bell pepper

2 tablespoons chopped onion

1½ teaspoons chopped fresh or ½ teaspoon dried basil leaves

½ teaspoon Worcestershire sauce

1 small tomato, coarsely chopped (about ½ cup)

1 clove garlic, finely chopped

½ can (16 ounces) garbanzo beans, rinsed and drained (about 1 cup)

1 can (8 ounces) kidney beans, rinsed and drained

1 cup chicken broth

Mix all ingredients in 2-quart saucepan. Heat to boiling, stirring occasionally; reduce heat. Cover and simmer about 15 minutes, stirring occasionally, until macaroni is tender. *2 servings.*

NUTRITION PER SERVING: Calories 360; Protein 22g; Carbohydrate 72g (Dietary Fiber 13g); Fat 4g (Unsaturated 3g, Saturated 1g); Cholesterol 0mg; Sodium 800mg.

PERCENT OF U.S. RDA: Vitamin A 4%; Vitamin C 10%; Calcium 8%; Iron 38%

Black Beans and Rice

Black Beans and Rice is one of the most popular Caribbean dishes. Try serving it with crusty bread or corn muffins.

1 slice bacon, cut into 1-inch pieces

1 small green bell pepper, chopped (about ½ cup)

1 small onion, chopped (about ¼ cup)

2 cloves garlic, finely chopped

1 cup chicken broth

⅓ cup uncooked regular long grain rice

¼ cup diced fully cooked smoked ham

¼ teaspoon pepper

¼ teaspoon red pepper sauce

1 medium tomato, chopped (about ¾ cup)

1 can (15 ounces) black beans, rinsed and drained

Cook bacon in 1½-quart saucepan over medium heat, stirring occasionally, until crisp. Remove bacon from saucepan with slotted spoon; drain. Reserve 1 tablespoon bacon fat in saucepan. Cook bell pepper, onion and garlic in bacon fat over medium heat about 3 minutes, stirring frequently, until vegetables are softened; drain.

Stir in bacon and remaining ingredients. Heat to boiling, stirring once or twice; reduce heat. Cover and simmer 14 minutes (do not lift cover or stir); remove from heat. Fluff with fork. Cover and let steam about 10 minutes or until rice is tender. *2 servings.*

NUTRITION PER SERVING: Calories 425; Protein 25g; Carbohydrate 79g (Dietary Fiber 14g); Fat 7g (Unsaturated 5g, Saturated 2g); Cholesterol 15mg; Sodium 1000mg.

PERCENT OF U.S. RDA: Vitamin A 6%; Vitamin C 30%; Calcium 14%; Iron 34%

Hot and Spicy Chile

You'll save yourself time later if you make a double batch of chile and freeze some for a rainy day.

4 ounces chorizo or bulk hot Italian sausage

1 small onion, chopped (about ¼ cup)

2 cloves garlic, finely chopped

1 can (8 ounces) stewed tomatoes

1 can (5½ ounces) spicy eight-vegetable juice

1 canned pickled jalapeño chile, rinsed, seeded and chopped (about 1 tablespoon)

1 tablespoon chopped fresh or 1 teaspoon dried oregano leaves

1½ teaspoons chile powder

¼ teaspoon ground cumin

1 can (15 to 16 ounces) red kidney beans, undrained

Sour cream, if desired

Cook sausage, onion and garlic in 2-quart saucepan over medium heat, stirring frequently, until sausage is brown; drain. Stir in remaining ingredients except beans and sour cream. Heat to boiling; reduce heat. Cover and simmer 20 minutes, stirring occasionally.

Stir in beans. Heat to boiling; reduce heat. Simmer uncovered about 20 minutes, stirring occasionally, until desired consistency. Top with sour cream. *2 servings.*

NUTRITION PER SERVING: Calories 600; Protein 37g; Carbohydrate 76g (Dietary Fiber 22g); Fat 26g (Unsaturated 17g, Saturated 9g); Cholesterol 50mg; Sodium 2100mg.

PERCENT OF U.S. RDA: Vitamin A 30%; Vitamin C 40%; Calcium 12%; Iron 54%

Hearty Lentil Soup

(Photograph on page 34)

2 cups chicken broth

1 can or bottle (12 ounces) beer or 1½ cups chicken broth

½ cup dried lentils, sorted and rinsed

1 medium carrot, sliced (about ½ cup)

1 medium stalk celery, chopped (about ½ cup)

1 small onion, chopped (about ¼ cup)

1 fully cooked smoked Polish sausage (about 5 inches long), thinly sliced (about 3 ounces)

1 tablespoon chopped fresh or 1 teaspoon dried basil leaves

⅛ teaspoon pepper

1 small bay leaf

2 tablespoons grated Parmesan cheese

Heat broth, beer and lentils to boiling in 2-quart saucepan; reduce heat. Cover and simmer 20 to 25 minutes, stirring occasionally, until lentils are tender but not mushy. Stir in remaining ingredients except cheese. Heat to boiling; reduce heat. Cover and simmer 20 minutes, stirring occasionally. Remove bay leaf. Sprinkle each serving with cheese. *2 servings.*

NUTRITION PER SERVING: Calories 365; Protein 29g; Carbohydrate 39g (Dietary Fiber 10g); Fat 15g (Unsaturated 10g, Saturated 5g); Cholesterol 30mg; Sodium 1820mg.

PERCENT OF U.S. RDA: Vitamin A 96%; Vitamin C *%; Calcium 16%; Iron 38%

CHAPTER
④
▰▰▰▰▰▰▰ MENUS ▰▰▰▰▰▰

LAZY DAY BRUNCH
Fresh-squeezed orange juice

Easy Huevos Rancheros (page 76)

Coffee cake

✖

BEAT-THE-COLD BREAKFAST
Fruit cup

Baked Egg Casserole (page 78)

Orange-Pecan Muffins (page 66)

Hot chocolate

✖

OCTOBERFEST FEAST
Swiss-Rye Strata (page 80)

German potato salad

Red cabbage slaw

Blueberry-Pear Crisps (page 98)

✖

SATURDAY TV BREAKFAST
Favorite fruit or juice

Breakfast Enchiladas (page 102)

Sweet rolls

REUNION DINNER
Gouda Puff (page 103)

Curried Asparagus (page 20)

Tossed salad

Strawberry shortcake

✖

COMPUTER GAMES GET-TOGETHER
Cheesy Vegetable Tortilla Rolls (page 106)

Sliced oranges

Chocolate brownie sundáes

✖

SUNDAY SUPPER
Potato-Cheese Soup (page 109)

Waldorf salad

Hard rolls

Peanut butter cookies

✖

"COMFORT FOODS" LUNCH
Grilled Three-Cheese Sandwiches (page 109)

Tomato bisque

Fresh apple wedges

Rice pudding

CHAPTER 4

EGGS AND CHEESE

Poached Eggs with Blue Cheese Sauce

Blue Cheese Sauce (right)

2 English muffins, split and toasted

2 tablespoons margarine or butter, softened

4 eggs

4 small sprigs parsley

Prepare Blue Cheese Sauce; keep warm. Spread muffin halves with margarine.

Heat water (about 1 inch) to boiling in 10-inch skillet; reduce heat to low. Break each egg, one at a time, into custard cup or saucer. Hold cup or saucer close to water's surface and slip egg into water. Cook 6 to 7 minutes or until whites are set and yolks are thickened. Remove eggs with slotted spoon.

Place 1 poached egg on each muffin half. Spoon sauce over eggs. Top with parsley. *2 servings.*

BLUE CHEESE SAUCE

1 tablespoon margarine or butter

2 to 3 medium green onions, sliced (about ¼ cup)

1 tablespoon all-purpose flour

⅔ cup milk

2 tablespoons crumbled blue or Gorgonzola cheese

Heat margarine in 1-quart saucepan over medium heat until melted. Cook onions in margarine about 3 minutes, stirring occasionally, until softened. Stir in flour. Cook over medium heat, stirring constantly, until smooth and bubbly; remove from heat. Stir in milk. Heat to boiling, stirring constantly. Boil and stir 1 minute. Stir in cheese until melted.

NUTRITION PER SERVING: Calories 510; Protein 22g; Carbohydrate 36g (Dietary Fiber 2g); Fat 32g (Unsaturated 23g, Saturated 9g); Cholesterol 440mg; Sodium 780mg.

PERCENT OF U.S. RDA: Vitamin A 44%; Vitamin C 6%; Calcium 30%; Iron 20%

Easy Huevos Rancheros

(Photograph on page 84)

2 flour tortillas (6 inches in diameter)

1 can (8 ounces) tomato sauce

¼ cup salsa

¼ teaspoon sugar

¼ teaspoon ground cumin

1 clove garlic, finely chopped

4 eggs

¼ cup shredded Colby-Monterey Jack cheese (1 ounce)

Heat oven to 350°. Wrap tortillas in aluminum foil. Heat about 10 minutes until warm. Remove tortillas from oven; keep wrapped.

Meanwhile, mix tomato sauce, salsa, sugar, cumin and garlic in 1-quart saucepan. Heat to boiling; reduce heat. Cover and simmer 5 minutes, stirring occasionally.

Heat water (1½ to 2 inches) to boiling in 10-inch skillet; reduce heat to low. Break each egg, one at a time, into custard cup or saucer. Hold cup or saucer close to water's surface and slip egg into water. Cook uncovered 6 to 7 minutes or until whites are set and yolks are thickened. Remove eggs with slotted spoon.

Place each warm tortilla on dinner plate. Top each tortilla with 2 poached eggs and the sauce. Sprinkle with cheese. *2 servings.*

NUTRITION PER SERVING: Calories 380; Protein 21g; Carbohydrate 37g (Dietary Fiber 3g); Fat 18g (Unsaturated 11g, Saturated 7g); Cholesterol 440mg; Sodium 1370mg.

PERCENT OF U.S. RDA: Vitamin A 30%; Vitamin C 28%; Calcium 18%; Iron 24%

Egg Salad Stacks

Keeping hard-cooked eggs on hand or buying them at the supermarket deli will speed up preparation.

2 English muffins, split, or 2 slices bread

4 hard-cooked eggs, chopped

2 medium green onions, sliced

¼ cup shredded carrot

2 tablespoons mayonnaise or salad dressing

2 tablespoons plain yogurt

¼ teaspoon curry powder

⅛ teaspoon salt

Dash of pepper

4 leaves romaine lettuce

4 rings yellow or green bell pepper

Alfalfa sprouts

Toast muffins. Mix eggs, onions, carrot, mayonnaise, yogurt, curry powder, salt and pepper. Place romaine leaves on muffin halves. Top with egg mixture, bell pepper rings and alfalfa sprouts. *2 servings.*

NUTRITION PER SERVING: Calories 405; Protein 19g; Carbohydrate 33g (Dietary Fiber 3g); Fat 23g (Unsaturated 18g, Saturated 5g); Cholesterol 435mg; Sodium 650mg.

PERCENT OF U.S. RDA: Vitamin A 46%; Vitamin C 20%; Calcium 20%; Iron 22%

Incredible Edible Eggs

Fast-to-fix eggs can be the basis for an easy main dish for two any meal of the day. Eggs are inexpensive, readily available and easy to keep on hand. Below are some basic directions for cooking eggs, plus some ideas for sparking them up.

Soft-cooked Eggs

Place eggs in saucepan. Add enough cold water to come at least 1 inch above eggs. Heat rapidly to boiling; remove from heat. Cover and let stand 3 minutes. Immediately cool eggs in cold water several seconds to prevent further cooking. Cut eggs into halves. Scoop eggs from shells.

Hard-cooked Eggs

Place eggs in saucepan. Add enough cold water to come at least 1 inch above eggs. Heat rapidly to boiling; remove from heat. Cover and let stand 18 minutes. Immediately cool eggs in cold water to prevent further cooking. Tap egg to crackle shell. Roll egg between hands to loosen shell, then peel. If shell is hard to peel, hold egg in cold water.

Poached Eggs

Heat water (1½ to 2 inches) to boiling; reduce to simmering. Break each egg into custard cup or saucer. Hold cup or saucer close to water's surface and slip egg into water. Cook about 5 minutes or until whites are set and yolks are thickened. Remove eggs with slotted spoon.

Fried Eggs

Heat margarine, butter or bacon fat (⅛ inch deep) in heavy skillet over medium heat. Break each egg into custard cup or saucer. Slip egg carefully into skillet. Immediately reduce heat to low. Cook 5 to 7 minutes, spooning margarine over eggs, until whites are set, a film forms over yolks and yolks are thickened. Or gently turn eggs over after 3 minutes and cook 1 to 2 minutes longer or until yolks are thickened.

Tips for Perking Up Basic Eggs

• Top poached or scrambled eggs with your favorite salsa or chutney.

• Keep hard-cooked eggs on hand to make sandwiches and main dishes or to top salads, vegetables and sauces.

• Make poached eggs special by using half dry white wine or chicken broth in the poaching liquid.

• Serve deviled eggs as a main course with steamed asparagus and sliced tomatoes.

Cheesy Asparagus Frittata

(Photograph on page 85)

4 eggs

¼ cup milk

¾ teaspoon chopped fresh or ¼ teaspoon dried chervil leaves

⅛ teaspoon salt

½ cup shredded Swiss or Havarti cheese (2 ounces)

2 tablespoons margarine or butter

¾ cup fresh or frozen (thawed) asparagus cuts

1 clove garlic, finely chopped

¼ cup chopped seeded tomato

Beat eggs, milk, chervil and salt in medium bowl until blended. Stir in cheese. Heat margarine in 8-inch ovenproof skillet over medium heat until melted. Cook asparagus and garlic in margarine about 3 minutes, stirring occasionally, until asparagus is crisp-tender. Stir in tomato; reduce heat to medium-low. Pour egg mixture over vegetables. Cover and cook about 9 minutes, without stirring, until eggs are set almost to center and are light brown on bottom. Remove cover.

Set oven control to broil. Broil frittata with top about 5 inches from heat about 2 minutes or until eggs are completely set and just starting to brown. *2 servings.*

NUTRITION PER SERVING: Calories 385; Protein 23g; Carbohydrate 7g (Dietary Fiber 1g); Fat 30g (Unsaturated 19g, Saturated 11g); Cholesterol 450mg; Sodium 480mg.

PERCENT OF U.S. RDA: Vitamin A 42%; Vitamin C 20%; Calcium 36%; Iron 10%

Baked Egg Casserole

You can also bake this homey casserole in a 8½×4½×2½-inch loaf pan.

1 cup garlic-flavored croutons

2 hard-cooked eggs, cut into halves

1 cup fresh or frozen (thawed and drained) broccoli cuts

½ cup shredded mozzarella cheese (2 ounces)

1 tablespoon margarine or butter

1 tablespoon all-purpose flour

1 teaspoon prepared horseradish

⅛ teaspoon pepper

1¼ cups milk

2 tablespoons grated Parmesan cheese

Heat oven to 350°. Arrange croutons evenly in 2 ungreased 10-ounce custard cups. Arrange egg halves and broccoli over croutons. Sprinkle with mozzarella cheese.

Heat margarine in 1-quart saucepan over medium heat until melted. Stir in flour, horseradish and pepper. Cook, stirring constantly, until smooth and bubbly; remove from heat. Stir in milk. Heat to boiling, stirring constantly. Boil and stir 1 minute. Pour evenly over mozzarella cheese.

Sprinkle with Parmesan cheese. Bake uncovered 20 to 25 minutes or until sauce is bubbly and center is hot. *2 servings.*

NUTRITION PER SERVING: Calories 425; Protein 27g; Carbohydrate 29g (Dietary Fiber 4g); Fat 24g (Unsaturated 12g, Saturated 12g); Cholesterol 245mg; Sodium 700mg.

PERCENT OF U.S. RDA: Vitamin A 44%; Vitamin C 30%; Calcium 56%; Iron 12%

Potato Breakfast Skillet

Crumbled cooked bacon or bacon bits are a delicious addition to this easy breakfast dish.

1 tablespoon margarine or butter

¾ cup frozen hash brown potatoes with onions and peppers

4 eggs, beaten

¼ cup milk

3 tablespoons grated Parmesan cheese

1 teaspoon chopped fresh or ¼ teaspoon dried oregano leaves

⅛ teaspoon red pepper sauce

¼ cup shredded Colby or mozzarella cheese (1 ounce)

Heat margarine in 8-inch skillet over medium heat until melted. Cook potatoes in margarine about 5 minutes, stirring frequently, until tender. Mix eggs, milk, Parmesan cheese, oregano and pepper sauce until blended; pour over potatoes.

Cook over medium heat, 3 to 4 minutes, without stirring, or until eggs are thickened throughout but still moist. As mixture begins to set at bottom and side, gently lift cooked portions with spatula so that thin, uncooked portion can flow to bottom. Sprinkle with Colby cheese. *2 servings.*

NUTRITION PER SERVING: Calories 410; Protein 21g; Carbohydrate 15g (Dietary Fiber 1g); Fat 30g (Unsaturated 19g, Saturated 11g); Cholesterol 450mg; Sodium 590mg.

PERCENT OF U.S. RDA: Vitamin A 28%; Vitamin C 8%; Calcium 26%; Iron 10%

Basil-Vegetable Scramble

2 cups cubed cooked potato (about 2 medium)

1 small onion, chopped (about ¼ cup)

½ small red bell pepper, chopped (about ¼ cup)

4 eggs

1 tablespoon chopped fresh or 1 teaspoon dried basil leaves

¼ teaspoon salt

⅛ teaspoon ground red pepper (cayenne)

Spray 10-inch nonstick skillet with nonstick cooking spray. Cook potatoes, onion and bell pepper in skillet over medium heat about 5 minutes, stirring occasionally, until hot. Mix remaining ingredients; pour into skillet.

Cook 2 to 4 minutes or until eggs are thickened throughout but still moist. As mixture begins to set at bottom and side, gently lift cooked portions with spatula so that thin, uncooked portion can flow to bottom. Avoid constant stirring. *2 servings.*

NUTRITION PER SERVING: Calories 290; Protein 16g; Carbohydrate 37g (Dietary Fiber 3g); Fat 10g (Unsaturated 7g, Saturated 3g); Cholesterol 430mg; Sodium 400mg.

PERCENT OF U.S. RDA: Vitamin A 20%; Vitamin C 20%; Calcium 8%; Iron 12%

Broccoli-Cheese Impossible Pies

Use your favorite frozen vegetable in these terrific cheese puffs.

½ cup frozen broccoli cuts, thawed and well drained

½ cup shredded brick or mozzarella cheese (2 ounces)

½ cup shredded Edam or Cheddar cheese (2 ounces)

½ cup milk

¼ cup Bisquick Original baking mix

1 egg

Heat oven to 350°. Grease two 10-ounce custard cups or individual casseroles. Divide broccoli between custard cups.

Place remaining ingredients in blender. Cover and blend on high speed about 15 seconds or until smooth. (Or beat ingredients on high speed 1 minute.) Pour mixture into custard cups. Bake 30 to 35 minutes or until knife inserted in center comes out clean. Cool 5 minutes before serving. *2 servings.*

NUTRITION PER SERVING: Calories 330; Protein 20g; Carbohydrate 14g (Dietary Fiber 1g); Fat 22g (Unsaturated 10g, Saturated 12g); Cholesterol 165mg; Sodium 730mg.

PERCENT OF U.S. RDA: Vitamin A 26%; Vitamin C 14%; Calcium 52%; Iron 6%

Swiss-Rye Strata

(Photograph on page 86)

2 teaspoons margarine or butter

2 tablespoons chopped onion

1 teaspoon chopped fresh or ¼ teaspoon dried thyme leaves

3 slices rye bread, cubed (about 2 cups)

¾ cup shredded Swiss or Havarti cheese (3 ounces)

¼ cup diced fully cooked smoked ham

2 eggs

1 cup milk

1 teaspoon Worcestershire sauce

⅛ teaspoon pepper

Heat margarine in 1-quart saucepan over medium heat until melted. Cook onion and thyme in margarine about 2 minutes, stirring frequently, until onion is softened.

Mix onion mixture, bread, cheese and ham. Divide bread mixture between 2 ungreased individual 16-ounce oval or round casseroles. Beat eggs in small bowl. Mix in remaining ingredients; pour over bread mixture. Cover and refrigerate at least 2 hours but no longer than 24 hours.

Heat oven to 325°. Bake uncovered 30 to 35 minutes or until knife inserted in center comes out clean. Let stand 5 minutes before serving. *2 servings.*

NUTRITION PER SERVING: Calories 455; Protein 29g; Carbohydrate 29g (Dietary Fiber 3g); Fat 26g (Unsaturated 14g, Saturated 12g); Cholesterol 270mg; Sodium 740mg.

PERCENT OF U.S. RDA: Vitamin A 26%; Vitamin C 8%; Calcium 60%; Iron 14%

▲ *Spinach-stuffed Pinwheels* (Recipe on page 62) and *Chocolate-Toffee Torte* (Recipe on page 99)

▲ *Herbed Lentils and Vegetables* (Recipe on page 70)

◄ *Cheese and Ham Tabbouleh Salad* (Recipe on page 71)

▲ *Cheesy Asparagus Frittata* (Recipe on page 78) and *Mediterranean Bread Crisps* (Recipe on page 67)

◄ *Easy Huevos Rancheros* (Recipe on page 76) and *Tex-Mex Corn Muffins* (Recipe on page 67)

▲ *French Omelet with Glazed Apples* (Recipe on page 97) and *Orange Pecan Muffins* (Recipe on page 66)

◄ *Swiss-Rye Strata* (Recipe on page 80) and *Fruity Coleslaw* (Recipe on page 53)

▲ *Cheesy Artichoke Calzones* (Recipe on page 108)

◄ *Mushroom Quiches* (Recipe on page 104)

▲ ***Southwestern Potato-Chicken Salad*** (Recipe on page 114) and ***Lemon Curd Parfaits*** (Recipe on page 98)

◄ ***Teriyaki Chicken Stir-Fry*** (Recipe on page 112)

▲ ***Shrimp-Pasta Salad Toss*** (Recipe on page 117) and ***Sesame Fingers*** (Recipe on page 67)

◄ ***Parsleyed Parmesan Fish*** (Recipe on page 116) and ***Hurry-Up Potato Salad*** (Recipe on page 52)

▲ *Feta-stuffed Lamb Patties* (Recipe on page 123) and *Zucchini-Couscous Salad* (Recipe on page 53)

◄ *Italian Kabobs* (Recipe on page 119)

Blue Cheese Quesadillas (Recipe on page 124) ►

French Omelet with Glazed Apples

(Photograph on page 87)

2 tablespoons packed brown sugar

1 tablespoon margarine or butter

1 large unpeeled red apple, sliced

⅓ cup ricotta cheese

⅓ cup shredded Cheddar cheese (1½ ounces)

4 eggs

2 tablespoons milk

2 teaspoons margarine or butter

2 teaspoons margarine or butter

Heat brown sugar and 1 tablespoon margarine to boiling in 1½-quart saucepan; reduce heat to medium. Stir in apple. Cook about 3 minutes, stirring frequently, until apple is crisp-tender. Remove from heat; keep warm. Mix ricotta cheese and Cheddar cheese.

Beat eggs and milk in medium bowl. Make 1 omelet at a time. Heat 2 teaspoons margarine in 8-inch omelet pan or skillet over medium-high heat just until margarine begins to brown. As margarine melts, tilt pan to coat bottom. Quickly pour half of the egg mixture into pan. Slide pan back and forth rapidly over heat and, at the same time, quickly stir with fork to spread eggs continuously over bottom of pan as they thicken. Let stand over heat a few seconds to set eggs and brown bottom of omelet lightly. (Do not overcook—omelet will continue to cook after folding.)

Tilt pan and run fork under edge of omelet, then jerk pan sharply to loosen from bottom of pan. Spoon half of the cheese mixture down center of omelet. Fold portion of omelet nearest you just to center. (Allow for portion of omelet to slide up side of pan.) Turn omelet onto warm plate, flipping folded portion of omelet over so far side is on bottom. Tuck sides of omelet under if necessary. Spoon half of the apple slices over omelet. *2 servings.*

NUTRITION PER SERVING: Calories 515; Protein 22g; Carbohydrate 34g (Dietary Fiber 2g); Fat 33g (Unsaturated 21g, Saturated 12g); Cholesterol 460mg; Sodium 460mg.

PERCENT OF U.S. RDA: Vitamin A 42%; Vitamin C 10%; Calcium 30%; Iron 12%

DELICIOUS DESSERTS

Sweets are lovely endings to any meal. While fresh fruit, ice cream, or packaged cookies are always quick-to-fix for two, these easy home-made desserts are an extra-special treat any time. Some are easily made from scratch, while others offer unusual twists to prepared foods. Enjoy!

Lemon Curd Parfaits

(Photograph on page 91)

½ cup lemon curd
2 tablespoons orange juice
1 cup whipped cream or frozen (thawed) whipped topping
8 chocolate wafer cookies
Raspberries, if desired

Mix lemon curd and orange juice in medium bowl. Fold in whipped cream. Coarsely crumble cookies; reserve 1 tablespoon crumbs. Layer half of the lemon curd mixture, the cookie crumbs and remaining lemon curd mixture in 2 parfait glasses. Sprinkle with reserved crumbs and top with raspberries. *2 servings.*

NUTRITION PER SERVING: Calories 455; Protein 2g; Carbohydrate 78g (Dietary Fiber 2g); Fat 16g (Unsaturated 6g, Saturated 10g); Cholesterol 16mg; Sodium 180mg.

PERCENT OF U.S. RDA: Vitamin A 2%; Vitamin C 20%; Calcium 2%; Iron 6%

Pineapple-Yogurt Shortcake

1 can (8 ounces) crushed pineapple in juice, drained
½ cup vanilla or pineapple yogurt
⅛ teaspoon ground mace

2 sponge shortcake cups
2 tablespoons chopped toasted pecans (page 8)

Mix pineapple, yogurt and mace; divide between shortcake cups. Sprinkle with pecans. *2 servings.*

NUTRITION PER SERVING: Calories 305; Protein 6g; Carbohydrate 57g (Dietary Fiber 2g); Fat 7g (Unsaturated 6g, Saturated 1g); Cholesterol 65mg; Sodium 130mg.

PERCENT OF U.S. RDA: Vitamin A 2%; Vitamin C 20%; Calcium 12%; Iron 6%

Blueberry-Pear Crisps

(Photograph on page 45)

1 small pear, peeled and coarsely chopped
½ cup fresh or frozen blueberries
2 tablespoons packed brown sugar
2 tablespoons whole wheat or all-purpose flour
1 tablespoon quick-cooking or regular oats
⅛ teaspoon apple pie spice or cinnamon
1 tablespoon firm margarine or butter
Cream or ice cream, if desired

Heat oven to 375°. Grease two 6-ounce custard or soufflé cups. Divide pear and blueberries between custard cups. Mix brown sugar, flour, oats and apple pie spice in small bowl. Cut in margarine with pastry blender until mixture is crumbly; sprinkle over fruit. Bake about 30 minutes or until topping is golden brown and pear is tender. Serve warm with cream or ice cream. *2 servings.*

NUTRITION PER SERVING: Calories 180; Protein 2g; Carbohydrate 32g (Dietary Fiber 3g); Fat 6g (Unsaturated 5g, Saturated 1g); Cholesterol 0mg; Sodium 75mg.

PERCENT OF U.S. RDA: Vitamin A 8%; Vitamin C 10%; Calcium 2%; Iron 4%

Individual Coconut Flans

In the summer, you can refrigerate these flans for a cool and creamy dessert.

> *2 tablespoons flaked coconut*
> *2 teaspoons caramel ice-cream topping*
> *¾ cup half-and-half*
> *3 tablespoons sugar*
> *¼ teaspoon vanilla*
> *Dash of ground allspice*
> *1 egg*
> *1 egg yolk*

Place 1 tablespoon coconut in each of 2 ungreased 6-ounce custard cups. Drizzle 1 teaspoon ice-cream topping over each. Beat remaining ingredients with hand beater or wire whisk; pour into custard cups.

Place round baking rack or steamer rack in 10-inch skillet. Place custard cups on rack. Pour boiling water into skillet until it comes almost to the top of the rack. (Water should not touch custard cups.) Cover skillet and steam over medium heat 11 to 12 minutes or until knife inserted halfway between center and edge comes out clean. (Watch flans closely the last few minutes of steaming.)

Remove cups from skillet; let stand 10 minutes. Loosen sides of flans from cups, using sharp knife. Unmold flans onto dessert plates. Serve warm. *2 servings.*

NUTRITION PER SERVING: Calories 310; Protein 7g; Carbohydrate 30g (Dietary Fiber 0g); Fat 18g (Unsaturated 8g, Saturated 10g); Cholesterol 250mg; Sodium 100mg.

PERCENT OF U.S. RDA: Vitamin A 16%; Vitamin C *%; Calcium 12%; Iron 4%

Chocolate-Toffee Torte

(Photograph on page 81)

You can add extra flair to this dessert by stacking the cake slices like steps.

> *½ cup soft-style cream cheese*
> *2 tablespoons powdered sugar*
> *1 tablespoon amaretto or ⅛ teaspoon almond extract*
> *1 bar (1.4 ounces) chocolate-covered toffee candy*
> *6 slices (about ¼ inch each) frozen pound cake, thawed*
> *¼ cup fudge ice-cream topping*

Mix cream cheese, powdered sugar and amaretto. Place candy bar in small plastic bag; seal bag. Coarsely crush candy with rolling pin.

Spread cream cheese mixture over 4 of the cake slices. Reserve 1 teaspoon of the crushed candy. Sprinkle remaining candy over cream cheese. For each serving, stack two of the cream cheese-topped cake slices. Top each stack with one of the remaining cake slices. Top each stack with dollop of ice-cream topping, spreading it slightly. Sprinkle with reserved candy. *2 servings.*

NUTRITION PER SERVING: Calories 585; Protein 7g; Carbohydrate 62g (Dietary Fiber 1g); Fat 35g (Unsaturated 16g, Saturated 19g); Cholesterol 120mg; Sodium 340mg.

PERCENT OF U.S. RDA: Vitamin A 16%; Vitamin C *%; Calcium 10%; Iron 10%

Puffy Omelet with Savory Zucchini Sauce

If you're not sure that the handle of your skillet is ovenproof, simply wrap it with a double thickness of aluminum foil.

> *4 eggs, separated*
> *¼ cup water*
> *¼ teaspoon salt*
> *1 tablespoon margarine or butter*
> *Savory Zucchini Sauce (right)*

Heat oven to 325°. Beat egg whites, water and salt in medium bowl on high speed until stiff but not dry. Beat egg yolks on high speed about 3 minutes or until very thick and lemon colored. Fold into egg whites.

Heat margarine in 10-inch ovenproof skillet over medium heat just until hot enough to sizzle a drop of water. As margarine melts, tilt skillet to coat bottom. Pour egg mixture into skillet. Level surface gently; reduce heat. Cook over low heat about 5 minutes or until puffy and bottom is light brown. (Lift omelet carefully at edge to judge color.) Bake uncovered 12 to 15 minutes or until knife inserted in center comes out clean.

Meanwhile, prepare Savory Zucchini Sauce. Tilt skillet and slip pancake turner or metal spatula under omelet to loosen. Fold omelet in half, being careful not to break it. Slip onto warm plate. Serve with sauce. *2 servings.*

SAVORY ZUCCHINI SAUCE

> *2 tablespoons margarine or butter*
> *⅓ cup shredded zucchini*
> *1 small onion, chopped (about ¼ cup)*
> *1 clove garlic, finely chopped*
> *2 tablespoons all-purpose flour*
> *1 teaspoon chopped fresh or ¼ teaspoon dried savory leaves*
> *Dash of salt*
> *Dash of pepper*
> *1 cup milk*

Heat margarine in 1-quart saucepan over medium heat until melted. Cook zucchini, onion and garlic in margarine about 3 minutes, stirring occasionally, until vegetables are softened. Stir in flour, savory, salt and pepper. Cook over medium heat, stirring constantly, until well blended and bubbly; remove from heat. Stir in milk. Heat to boiling, stirring constantly. Boil and stir 1 minute.

NUTRITION PER SERVING: Calories 410; Protein 18g; Carbohydrate 18g (Dietary Fiber 1g); Fat 30g (Unsaturated 22g, Saturated 8g); Cholesterol 435mg; Sodium 790mg.

PERCENT OF U.S. RDA: Vitamin A 46%; Vitamin C 8%; Calcium 22%; Iron 12%

TAILORED FOR TWO
Cheese, Please

Whether you serve cheese as an appetizer for two, sprinkle it over pasta, or serve it with fruit, you know that cheese is a great addition to any meal. Here are some helpful suggestions for cooking and eating cheese:

• Serve natural cheeses at room temperature to bring out their fullest flavor. Let stand covered about 30 minutes.

• Keep cooking temperatures low and cooking times short. High heat and overcooking cause cheese to become stringy and tough.

• When adding cheese to hot foods, cut into small pieces so it melts evenly and quickly.

• Cheese can be frozen, but expect the texture to change slightly—it will be more crumbly. Shred leftover cheese before freezing.

• To vary cottage cheese, stir in one of these easy-to-prepare combinations: shredded carrots and raisins; crushed pineapple and fresh mint; chopped green bell pepper, tomato and onion; sunflower nuts, alfalfa sprouts and chopped carrots; or toasted pine nuts, chopped tomato and basil.

• Mix preserves or jam into cottage cheese or cream cheese. Spread on toast or English muffins and broil.

• Spread prepared pesto on the inside of both slices of bread when making a grilled-cheese sandwich.

• Sprinkle the buttered sides of a grilled-cheese sandwich with Parmesan cheese for an extra cheesy flavor and a crispier crust.

Egg-topped Pita Pizzas

2 pita breads (4 or 6 inches in diameter)
½ cup sour cream–and-onion dip
1 teaspoon chopped fresh or ¼ teaspoon dried dill weed
1 tablespoon margarine or butter
¼ cup chopped celery
¼ cup shredded carrot
4 eggs
¼ cup milk
⅛ teaspoon salt
⅛ teaspoon pepper
¼ cup shredded Cheddar cheese (1 ounce)

Heat oven to 425°. Split each pita bread in half around edge, using knife. Place cut side up on ungreased cookie sheet. Bake uncovered about 5 minutes or just until crisp.

Meanwhile, mix sour cream dip and dill weed. Heat margarine in 10-inch skillet over medium heat until melted. Cook celery and carrot in margarine about 3 minutes, stirring occasionally, until celery is tender. Mix eggs, milk, salt and pepper; pour into skillet.

Cook 2 to 3 minutes or until eggs are thickened throughout but still moist. As mixture begins to set at bottom and side, gently lift cooked portions with spatula so that thin, uncooked portion can flow to bottom. Avoid constant stirring.

Spread dip mixture on baked pita rounds. Top with egg mixture. Sprinkle with cheese. Bake about 5 minutes or until cheese is melted. *2 servings.*

NUTRITION PER SERVING: Calories 460; Protein 22g; Carbohydrate 24g (Dietary Fiber 1g); Fat 31g (Unsaturated 17g, Saturated 14g); Cholesterol 480mg; Sodium 1010mg.

PERCENT OF U.S. RDA: Vitamin A 78%; Vitamin C 2%; Calcium 26%; Iron 14%

Breakfast Enchiladas

1 tablespoon margarine or butter

1 cup sliced mushrooms (about 3 ounces)

4 eggs

2 tablespoons chopped fresh parsley

¼ teaspoon salt

⅛ teaspoon pepper

4 flour tortillas (6 inches in diameter)

Pepper Cheese Sauce (below)

¼ cup chopped tomato

Heat oven to 350°. Grease square baking dish, 8×8×2 inches, or rectangular baking dish, 11×7×1½ inches. Heat margarine in 10-inch skillet over medium heat until melted. Cook mushrooms in margarine about 3 minutes, stirring frequently, until tender. Beat eggs, parsley, salt and pepper; pour into skillet.

Cook about 4 minutes or until eggs are thickened throughout but still moist. As mixture begins to set at bottom and side, gently lift cooked portions with spatula so that thin, uncooked portion can flow to bottom. Avoid constant stirring.

Spoon egg mixture onto center of each tortilla. Roll tortillas around egg mixture and place seam side down in baking dish. Prepare Pepper Cheese Sauce. Pour sauce over enchiladas in baking dish. Cover with aluminum foil and bake about 20 minutes or until sauce is bubbly. Sprinkle with tomato. *2 servings.*

PEPPER CHEESE SAUCE

1 tablespoon margarine or butter

1 tablespoon all-purpose flour

¾ cup milk

½ cup shredded hot pepper cheese (2 ounces)

Heat margarine in 1-quart saucepan over medium heat until melted. Stir in flour. Cook over medium heat, stirring constantly, until smooth and bubbly; remove from heat. Stir in milk. Heat to boiling, stirring constantly. Boil and stir 1 minute. Stir in cheese until melted.

NUTRITION PER SERVING: Calories 705; Protein 31g; Carbohydrate 61g (Dietary Fiber 4g); Fat 39g (Unsaturated 25g, Saturated 14g); Cholesterol 465mg; Sodium 1070mg.

PERCENT OF U.S. RDA: Vitamin A 48%; Vitamin C 22%; Calcium 42%; Iron 36%

Quick Chile-Cheese Puff

½ cup shredded sharp Cheddar cheese (2 ounces)

1 can (4 ounces) whole green chiles, drained

¼ cup milk

2 tablespoons all-purpose flour

⅛ teaspoon pepper

1 egg

Heat oven to 350°. Lightly grease two 10-ounce custard cups. Layer half of the cheese, the chiles and remaining cheese in custard cups. Beat remaining ingredients with hand beater until smooth; pour over top. Bake about 20 minutes or until puffy and golden brown. *2 servings.*

NUTRITION PER SERVING: Calories 200; Protein 12g; Carbohydrate 11g (Dietary Fiber 0g); Fat 12g (Unsaturated 5g, Saturated 7g); Cholesterol 135mg; Sodium 700mg.

PERCENT OF U.S. RDA: Vitamin A 14%; Vitamin C 20%; Calcium 20%; Iron 6%

Gouda Puff

Because this puff is like a soufflé, don't waste a minute bringing it to the table.

> *¾ cup shredded Gouda or Edam cheese (3 ounces)*
>
> *¼ cup all-purpose flour*
>
> *½ cup milk*
>
> *2 tablespoons margarine or butter, melted*
>
> *1 tablespoon chopped fresh or 1 teaspoon freeze-dried chives*
>
> *⅛ teaspoon lemon pepper*
>
> *2 eggs*

Heat oven to 350°. Grease two 10-ounce custard cups or individual soufflé dishes. Beat all ingredients on medium speed until well blended.

Carefully pour egg mixture into custard cups. Bake 30 to 35 minutes or until knife inserted halfway between center and edge comes out clean. Serve immediately. *2 servings.*

NUTRITION PER SERVING: Calories 415; Protein 20g; Carbohydrate 16g (Dietary Fiber 0g); Fat 30g (Unsaturated 18g, Saturated 12g); Cholesterol 255mg; Sodium 640mg.

PERCENT OF U.S. RDA: Vitamin A 38%; Vitamin C 2%; Calcium 42%; Iron 10%

Triple Cheese Ravioli

> *4 ounces dried cheese-filled ravioli or tortellini (about 1 cup)*
>
> *½ cup sliced mushrooms (about 1½ ounces)*
>
> *2 tablespoons chopped onion*
>
> *1 tablespoon chopped fresh or 1 teaspoon dried basil leaves*
>
> *2 tablespoons dry red wine or chicken broth*
>
> *Dash of salt*
>
> *Dash of pepper*
>
> *1 large tomato, chopped (about 1 cup)*
>
> *1 clove garlic, finely chopped*
>
> *½ cup ricotta cheese*
>
> *2 tablespoons grated Parmesan cheese*

Cook ravioli as directed on package; drain. Cook remaining ingredients except cheeses in 10-inch skillet over medium-high heat about 5 minutes, stirring frequently, until tomato is soft.

Heat oven to 325°. Place ravioli in ungreased loaf dish, 9×5×3 inches. Spread ricotta cheese over ravioli. Pour tomato sauce over top. Sprinkle with Parmesan cheese. Bake uncovered about 20 minutes or until hot. *2 servings.*

NUTRITION PER SERVING: Calories 465; Protein 29g; Carbohydrate 42g (Dietary Fiber 4g); Fat 22g (Unsaturated 11g, Saturated 11g); Cholesterol 205mg; Sodium 620mg.

PERCENT OF U.S. RDA: Vitamin A 26%; Vitamin C 10%; Calcium 60%; Iron 24%

Mushroom Quiches

(Photograph on page 88)

Be sure to use deep (about 1-inch) quiche dishes or tart pans so all the filling fits.

Easy Pastry (below)

*½ cup shredded mozzarella cheese
   (2 ounces)*

½ cup sliced mushrooms (about 1½ ounces)

2 tablespoons chopped green bell pepper

1 tablespoon chopped pepperoni

1 egg

½ cup milk

2 tablespoons grated Parmesan cheese

1 teaspoon chopped fresh or ¼ teaspoon dried basil leaves

Heat oven to 350°. Prepare Easy Pastry. Divide pastry into halves. Pat pastry firmly and evenly on bottoms and completely up sides of 2 deep individual 4-inch quiche dishes or tart pans or ungreased 10-ounce custard cups. Bake 15 to 20 minutes or until light brown.

Meanwhile, mix mozzarella cheese, mushrooms, bell pepper and pepperoni. Divide cheese mixture between baked crusts. Beat egg slightly in small bowl. Beat in remaining ingredients; pour into crusts. Bake about 25 minutes or until knife inserted in center comes out clean. Let stand 5 minutes before serving. *2 servings.*

EASY PASTRY

⅔ cup all-purpose flour

¼ cup (½ stick) margarine or butter, softened

1 egg yolk

Mix all ingredients until flour is well blended. Gather pastry into a ball.

NUTRITION PER SERVING: Calories 580; Protein 22g; Carbohydrate 39g (Dietary Fiber 2g); Fat 38g (Unsaturated 27g, Saturated 11g); Cholesterol 240mg; Sodium 650mg.

PERCENT OF U.S. RDA: Vitamin A 46%; Vitamin C 10%; Calcium 38%; Iron 18%

TAILORED FOR TWO
Deluxe Dining

Creating a fun, fancy or flamboyant meal for two, whether breakfast, lunch or dinner, can be more interesting than cooking for 4, 6, or larger numbers of people. The smaller number makes it easier to justify a splurge here and there for dinnerware, flatware and table linens. These tips can help your table be fashionable as well as affordable.

• Theme your meals and coordinate the table settings accordingly.

• Choose a dining location that suits the meal and the mood. Try the family room, the coffee table, the garden, porch or backyard.

• Shop for 2 place settings of different dishes along with matching table linens.

• Snap up those interesting placemats and napkins for great prices during "white sales" and seasonal closeouts.

• Use a beach towel for a tablecloth and terry hand towels for napkins when serving messier foods like barbecued ribs or fried chicken. These linens are a breeze to wash!

• Use brown wrapping paper to cover the table, and provide crayons for mealtime doodling or storytelling.

Three-Cheese Fondue

½ cup shredded Swiss cheese (2 ounces)

½ cup shredded Colby cheese (2 ounces)

*½ cup shredded Monterey Jack cheese
  (2 ounces)*

2 teaspoons cornstarch

1 clove garlic, cut into halves

½ cup dry white wine or white grape juice

*2 tablespoons dry sherry or kirsch or
  1 teaspoon sherry extract*

¼ teaspoon ground ginger

Several dashes of red pepper sauce

Bread cubes or vegetable dippers

Toss cheeses and cornstarch. Rub garlic on bottom and side of heavy 1-quart saucepan. Add white wine. Heat over low heat just until bubbles rise to surface. (Wine should not boil.)

Gradually add cheeses, about ¼ cup at a time, stirring constantly with wooden spoon over low heat until cheeses melt. Stir in sherry, ginger and pepper sauce. Remove to earthenware fondue dish; keep warm over low heat. Spear bread cubes with fondue forks. Dip and swirl in fondue with stirring motion. If fondue becomes too thick, stir in small amount of heated wine. *2 servings.*

NUTRITION PER SERVING: Calories 415; Protein 24g; Carbohydrate 22g (Dietary Fiber 1g); Fat 26g (Unsaturated 10g, Saturated 16g); Cholesterol 80mg; Sodium 580mg.

PERCENT OF U.S. RDA: Vitamin A 18%; Vitamin C *%; Calcium 64%; Iron 8%

Vegetable Rarebit Cups

You can buy prebaked pastry shells at a bakery, or unbaked shells in the frozen foods section of your supermarket. Follow the directions on the package to bake.

*2 cups frozen mixed broccoli, cauliflower
  and carrots*

2 tablespoons margarine or butter

2 tablespoons all-purpose flour

1 teaspoon Dijon mustard

¾ cup milk

*2 tablespoons dry white wine or chicken
  broth*

*1 cup shredded Fontina or Cheddar
  cheese (4 ounces)*

2 baked puff pastry shells

Cook vegetables as directed on package; drain well.

Heat margarine in 1½-quart saucepan over medium heat until melted. Stir in flour and mustard. Cook over medium heat, stirring constantly, until smooth and bubbly; remove from heat. Stir in milk. Heat to boiling, stirring constantly. Boil and stir 1 minute. Stir in wine. Gradually stir in cheese until melted. Fold in vegetables. Serve over pastry shells. *2 servings.*

NUTRITION PER SERVING: Calories 470; Protein 20g; Carbohydrate 25g (Dietary Fiber 4g); Fat 34g (Unsaturated 19g, Saturated 15g); Cholesterol 60mg; Sodium 670mg.

PERCENT OF U.S. RDA: Vitamin A 100%; Vitamin C 50%; Calcium 56%; Iron 10%

Cheesy Vegetable Tortilla Rolls

If you prefer, you may use crepes (either home-made or store-bought) instead of the tortillas.

1 tablespoon margarine or butter

1 cup fresh or frozen (thawed) asparagus cuts

¼ cup drained canned sliced water chestnuts

1 small onion, chopped (about ¼ cup)

1 tablespoon margarine or butter

1 tablespoon all-purpose flour

¾ teaspoon chopped fresh or ¼ teaspoon dried tarragon leaves

⅛ teaspoon salt

⅛ teaspoon pepper

1 cup milk

1½ teaspoons chopped fresh or ½ teaspoon freeze-dried chives

1 cup shredded Swiss cheese (4 ounces)

4 flour tortillas (6 inches in diameter)

Heat oven to 350°. Grease square baking dish, 8×8×2 inches. Heat 1 tablespoon margarine in 10-inch skillet over medium heat until melted. Cook asparagus, water chestnuts and onion in margarine about 2 minutes, stirring frequently, until vegetables are crisp-tender; remove from heat.

Heat 1 tablespoon margarine in 1-quart saucepan over medium heat until melted. Stir in flour, tarragon, salt and pepper. Cook, stirring constantly, until smooth and bubbly; remove from heat. Stir in milk. Heat to boiling, stirring constantly. Boil and stir 1 minute. Stir in chives and cheese.

Stir ½ cup sauce into vegetables. Spoon one-fourth of the vegetable mixture onto center of each tortilla. Roll each tortilla around vegetable mixture and place seam side down in baking dish. Pour remaining sauce over tortillas. Cover with aluminum foil and bake about 20 minutes or until tortillas are hot and sauce is bubbly. *2 servings.*

NUTRITION PER SERVING: Calories 670; Protein 28g; Carbohydrate 65g (Dietary Fiber 4g); Fat 35g (Unsaturated 19g, Saturated 16g); Cholesterol 65mg; Sodium 790mg.

PERCENT OF U.S. RDA: Vitamin A 36%; Vitamin C 20%; Calcium 74%; Iron 22%

Vegetarian Pizza

Broccoli slaw is julienned strips of fresh broccoli stalks mixed with shredded red cabbage and carrots. Look for it in the produce department right near the coleslaw mix.

Crust (page 108)

½ cup pizza sauce

1 cup broccoli slaw

1 cup sliced mushrooms

¼ cup chopped green or red bell pepper

1 cup shredded Italian-style four-cheese combination or mozzarella cheese (4 ounces)

Heat oven to 425°. Grease cookie sheet. Prepare Crust. Divide dough for crust into halves. Pat each half into 6-inch circle on cookie sheet, using floured fingers. Build up edges of circles slightly. Bake 10 minutes or until crusts start to brown. Spread pizza sauce over crusts. Top with broccoli slaw, mushrooms and bell pepper. Sprinkle with cheese. Bake 15 to 20 minutes or until heated through. *2 servings.*

NUTRITION PER SERVING: Calories 570; Protein 30g; Carbohydrate 77g (Dietary Fiber 9g); Fat 20g (Unsaturated 12g, Saturated 8g); Cholesterol 30mg; Sodium 710mg.

PERCENT OF U.S. RDA: Vitamin A 30%; Vitamin C 50%; Calcium 50%; Iron 38%

Savory Mushroom Puffs

Savory Mushroom Puffs are an extra special treat. The puffs can be made a day ahead and stored loosely covered if desired.

½ cup water

¼ cup (½ stick) margarine or butter

½ cup all-purpose flour

2 eggs

½ cup shredded process Swiss cheese (2 ounces)

1 teaspoon chopped fresh or ¼ teaspoon dried thyme leaves

¼ teaspoon ground mustard

Swiss-Mushroom Sauce (right)

Heat oven to 400°. Heat water and margarine to rolling boil in 1½-quart saucepan. Stir in flour; reduce heat. Stir vigorously about 1 minute or until mixture forms a ball; remove from heat. Beat in eggs all at once. Continue beating until smooth. Stir in cheese, thyme and mustard. Drop dough into 4 mounds onto ungreased cookie sheet. Bake 30 to 35 minutes or until puffs are dry and golden brown.

Meanwhile, prepare Swiss-Mushroom Sauce. Cut off top one-third of puffs and pull out any filaments of soft dough. Fill puffs with sauce. *2 servings.*

SWISS-MUSHROOM SAUCE

1 tablespoon margarine or butter

2 cups sliced mushrooms (about 6 ounces)

2 tablespoons chopped fresh or 2 teaspoons freeze-dried chives

1 tablespoon all-purpose flour

¼ teaspoon salt

⅛ teaspoon lemon pepper

1 cup milk

½ cup shredded process Swiss cheese (2 ounces)

Heat margarine in 10-inch skillet over medium-low heat until melted. Stir in mushrooms and chives. Cover and cook until mushrooms are tender. Stir in flour, salt and lemon pepper. Cook over medium heat, stirring constantly, until well blended and bubbly; remove from heat. Stir in milk. Heat to boiling, stirring constantly. Boil and stir 1 minute. Stir in cheese until melted.

NUTRITION PER SERVING: Calories 740; Protein 32g; Carbohydrate 43g (Dietary Fiber 5g); Fat 51g (Unsaturated 33g, Saturated 18g); Cholesterol 270mg; Sodium 1500mg.

PERCENT OF U.S. RDA: Vitamin A 64%; Vitamin C 14%; Calcium 64%; Iron 32%

Cheesy Artichoke Calzones

(*Photograph on page 89*)

If you'd like a milder flavor, use mozzarella or provolone cheese instead of the Cheddar.

Crust (below)

*1 jar (6 ounces) marinated artichoke
    hearts*

*½ cup shredded Cheddar cheese
    (2 ounces)*

*½ cup soft-style cream cheese with chives
    and onion*

*¼ cup julienne strips or diced fully
    cooked smoked ham*

*1 tablespoon fresh chopped or 1 teaspoon
    dried oregano leaves*

Heat oven to 375°. Grease cookie sheet. Prepare Crust. Drain artichokes well, reserving 1 table-spoon marinade. Coarsely chop artichokes. Mix artichokes, reserved marinade and remaining ingredients.

Divide dough for crust into halves. Pat each half into 8-inch circle on cookie sheet, using floured fingers. Spoon artichoke mixture onto half of each dough circle. Moisten edges of dough circles with water. Fold dough over filling. Seal edges by pressing with tines of fork. Bake 30 to 35 minutes or until crust is golden brown. *2 servings.*

CRUST

*1 package regular or quick-acting active
    dry yeast*

½ cup warm water (105° to 115°)

1¼ cups all-purpose flour

1 tablespoon olive or vegetable oil

⅛ teaspoon salt

Dissolve yeast in warm water in medium bowl. Stir in remaining ingredients. Beat vigorously 20 strokes. Let rest 5 minutes. Knead in enough flour to make dough easy to handle.

NUTRITION PER SERVING: Calories 750; Protein 27g; Carbohydrate 72g (Dietary Fiber 6g); Fat 42g (Unsaturated 21g, Saturated 21g); Cholesterol 105mg; Sodium 900mg.

PERCENT OF U.S. RDA: Vitamin A 24%; Vitamin C 18%; Calcium 24%; Iron 36%

TAILORED FOR TWO
Menu-Making

Add some life to your menus by taking a bit of time to plan lively meals. When you plan a menu, consider the *entire* day. You may choose to have 2 meals plus snacks rather than the typical three meals a day, or you can eat the heaviest meal at noon.

• Choose foods with a variety of flavors, textures, colors, shapes and temperatures.

• Choose the main course first. Whether meat or meatless, the rest of the meal can be easily planned around it.

• Use easy and convenient prepared foods such as salsas, relishes, marinades and sauces to add flavor to plain foods. These are readily available off the shelf or in the refrigerated section of your supermarket.

• Eat less than 30% of total calories from fat and get plenty of complex carbohydrates and fiber. Emphasis should be on grain foods like whole-grain breads and cereals, lots of different vegetables and fruits, moderate amounts of lowfat dairy foods, lean meats and only a few fats and sweets each day.

Grilled Three-Cheese Sandwiches

4 slices rye or white bread

2 tablespoons prepared pesto or spicy mustard

1 tablespoon sunflower nuts

1 slice (1½ ounces) mozzarella cheese, cut into halves

1 slice (1½ ounces) Swiss cheese, cut into halves

1 slice (1½ ounces) Cheddar cheese, cut into halves, or 2 slices (¾ ounce each) process American cheese

2 tablespoons margarine or butter, softened

Spread 1 side of each slice bread with pesto. Sprinkle sunflower nuts over pesto on 2 slices bread. For each sandwich, place 1 piece each of mozzarella cheese, Swiss cheese and Cheddar cheese on top of the sunflower nuts. Top with remaining bread, pesto side down. Spread tops of bread with half of the margarine.

Place sandwiches, margarine side down, in 10-inch skillet. Spread tops of bread with remaining margarine. Cook uncovered over medium heat about 5 minutes or until golden brown. Turn and cook 2 to 3 minutes or until golden brown and cheese is melted. *2 servings.*

NUTRITION PER SERVING: Calories 520; Protein 23g; Carbohydrate 28g (Dietary Fiber 4g); Fat 37g (Unsaturated 23g, Saturated 14g); Cholesterol 55mg; Sodium 890mg.

PERCENT OF U.S. RDA: Vitamin A 26%; Vitamin C *%; Calcium 54%; Iron 12%

Potato-Cheese Soup

¾ cup chicken broth

1 large potato, chopped (about 1 cup)

1 tablespoon margarine or butter

½ cup sliced leek

1 tablespoon all-purpose flour

1½ teaspoons chopped fresh or ½ teaspoon dried marjoram leaves

1¼ cups milk

1 cup shredded brick or Cheddar cheese (4 ounces)

¼ cup croutons

Heat broth to boiling in 1-quart saucepan. Stir in potato. Heat to boiling; reduce heat. Cover and simmer 10 minutes, stirring occasionally, until potato is tender.

Meanwhile, heat margarine in 1½-quart saucepan over medium heat until melted. Cook leek in margarine about 3 minutes, stirring frequently, until leek is tender. Stir in flour and marjoram. Stir in potato with broth and the milk. Heat to boiling over medium heat, stirring constantly. Boil and stir 1 minute. Stir in cheese; reduce heat. Heat, stirring constantly, just until cheese is melted. Sprinkle with croutons. *2 servings.*

NUTRITION PER SERVING: Calories 470; Protein 23g; Carbohydrate 37g (Dietary Fiber 3g); Fat 27g (Unsaturated 12g, Saturated 15g); Cholesterol 65mg; Sodium 850mg.

PERCENT OF U.S. RDA: Vitamin A 46%; Vitamin C 20%; Calcium 62%; Iron 12%

CHAPTER ⑤

▝▚▝▚▝▚▝▚▝ MENUS ▝▚▝▚▝▚▝

APPLE HARVEST DINNER

Chicken with Apple Butter Sauce (page 111)

Julienne carrots with sugar snap peas

Zucchini-Couscous Salad (page 53)

Bread pudding with caramel sauce

✖

AFTER THE ZOO

Mini Turkey Loaves (page 113)

Sweet-and-Sour Vegetable Stir-fry
(page 20)

Hard rolls

Chocolate cake with ice cream

✖

RAINY DAY DINNER

Parsleyed Parmesan Fish (page 116)

Acorn squash

Creamy Vegetable Salad (page 53)

Peach cobbler

✖

LUNCH ON THE DECK

Crab-Dijon Sandwiches (page 118)

Sliced fresh fruit

Individual Coconut Flans (page 99)

CHINESE NEW YEAR CELEBRATION

Five-Spice Meatballs (page 118)

White rice

Sesame Vegetable Medley (page 21)

Shredded lettuce with mandarin oranges

Orange sherbet • fortune cookies

Hot tea

✖

ART FAIR FINALE

Gyros-style Lamb Chops (page 122)

Mixed vegetables

Orange Salad with Blackberry Dressing
(page 52)

Mint ice cream • vanilla wafers

✖

GAME-TIME GRUB

Zesty Barbecue Sandwiches (page 123)

Potato chips

Celery and carrot sticks with dip

Ice cream bars

✖

ROUGH DAY AT THE OFFICE

Blue Cheese Quesadillas (page 124)

Tomato wedges

Pineapple-Yogurt Shortcake (page 98)

CHAPTER 5

WHEN TIME COUNTS

Chicken with Apple Butter Sauce

2 skinless boneless chicken breast halves (about ½ pound)

1 tablespoon margarine or butter, melted

1 medium apple, sliced

3 tablespoons apple butter

1 tablespoon orange juice

Ground cinnamon

Set oven control to broil. Grease broiler pan rack. Place chicken breast halves on rack in broiler pan. Brush chicken with about half of the margarine. Broil with tops 4 inches from heat about 6 minutes or until chicken just starts to brown.

Arrange apple slices in single layer on rack with chicken. Turn chicken; brush apple slices and chicken with remaining margarine. Broil 5 to 6 minutes longer or until chicken is brown on outside and juices are no longer pink when center of thickest piece is cut. Mix apple butter and orange juice.

Remove apple slices to dinner plates; sprinkle with cinnamon. Spoon apple butter mixture over chicken. Broil 1 minute longer. Serve chicken with apple slices. *2 servings.*

NUTRITION PER SERVING: Calories 275; Protein 26g; Carbohydrate 24g (Dietary Fiber 2g); Fat 9g (Unsaturated 7g, Saturated 2g); Cholesterol 65mg; Sodium 130mg.

PERCENT OF U.S. RDA: Vitamin A 8%; Vitamin C *%; Calcium 2%; Iron 6%

Smart Shopping

You'll find that supermarkets are stocking foods specifically packaged to meet the needs of smaller households more and more. Here are some shopping tips that will set you off on the right foot.

• Consider the amount of cupboard, refrigerator and freezer space available before you begin shopping.

• Shop in stores where meats and produce can be purchased "by the piece" rather than only "by the package."

• Use the deli or salad bar to purchase cut-up vegetables and meats for casseroles and pasta salads.

• Share shopping with a friend who also cooks for two. Split those foods that come packaged for 4.

• Purchase spices and herbs in the smallest containers possible so they are used up quickly.

• Create menus for a few days or a week and make a shopping list to avoid overspending.

• Look for canned and frozen vegetables and frozen entrées that come in servings for two.

• If you buy ground meat in 1-pound amounts, repackage it before refrigerating or freezing.

Teriyaki Chicken Stir-fry

(Photograph on page 90)

For best stir-frying results, make sure that the vegetables and chicken are well drained. If you have the time, make quick-cooking brown rice to go with this flavorful stir-fry.

½ pound skinless boneless chicken breast halves

1 tablespoon vegetable oil

1 tablespoon vegetable oil

1 cup frozen (thawed) crinkle-cut or sliced carrots

1 cup frozen (thawed) asparagus cuts

3 tablespoons teriyaki sauce

3 tablespoons water

Cut chicken breast halves into bite-size pieces. Heat wok or 10-inch skillet over high heat until 1 or 2 drops of water bubble and skitter when sprinkled in wok. Add 1 tablespoon oil; rotate wok to coat side. Add chicken; stir-fry about 4 minutes or until no longer pink in center. Remove chicken from wok.

Add 1 tablespoon oil to wok; rotate wok to coat side. Add carrots and asparagus; stir-fry 3 to 4 minutes or until vegetables are crisp-tender. Stir in teriyaki sauce and water. Cook and stir until bubbly. Stir in chicken. Cook and stir until heated through. *2 servings.*

NUTRITION PER SERVING: Calories 320; Protein 30g; Carbohydrate 15g (Dietary Fiber 3g); Fat 17g (Unsaturated 14g, Saturated 3g); Cholesterol 65mg; Sodium 1150mg.

PERCENT OF U.S. RDA: Vitamin A 100%; Vitamin C 20%; Calcium 6%; Iron 12%

Turkey and Rice Olé

½ pound turkey breast slices or boneless, skinless chicken breast halves

½ cup uncooked instant rice

1 tablespoon olive or vegetable oil

½ cup chunky salsa

½ cup shredded Cheddar cheese (2 ounces)

Cut turkey into bite-size pieces. Cook rice as directed on package. Meanwhile, heat oil in 10-inch skillet over medium heat until hot. Cook turkey in oil about 4 minutes, stirring frequently, until no longer pink in center; drain. Stir cooked rice and salsa into turkey in skillet; heat through. Sprinkle with cheese; reduce heat. Cover and cook 1 to 2 minutes or until cheese is melted. *2 servings.*

NUTRITION PER SERVING: Calories 475; Protein 44g; Carbohydrate 29g (Dietary Fiber 1g); Fat 21g (Unsaturated 13g, Saturated 8g); Cholesterol 115mg; Sodium 1200mg.

PERCENT OF U.S. RDA: Vitamin A 10%; Vitamin C *%; Calcium 18%; Iron 16%

Mini Turkey Loaves

½ pound ground turkey

¼ cup plus 2 tablespoons quick-cooking oats

¼ cup shredded sharp Cheddar cheese (1 ounce)

¼ cup milk

2 tablespoons chopped onion

¼ teaspoon salt

¼ teaspoon ground mustard

⅛ teaspoon pepper

¼ cup Russian dressing, barbecue sauce or chile sauce

Heat oven to 350°. Mix all ingredients except dressing. Shape mixture into 2 loaves. Place loaves in greased square pan, 8×8×2 or 9×9×2 inches, or round pan, 8 or 9×1½ inches. Brush half of the dressing over loaves. Bake uncovered 30 to 35 minutes or until no longer pink in center. Brush with remaining dressing. Let stand 5 minutes before serving. *2 servings.*

NUTRITION PER SERVING: Calories 480; Protein 30g; Carbohydrate 16g (Dietary Fiber 2g); Fat 34g (Unsaturated 25g, Saturated 9g); Cholesterol 100mg; Sodium 710mg.

PERCENT OF U.S. RDA: Vitamin A 8%; Vitamin C *%; Calcium 14%; Iron 14%

Creamy Chicken Soup

1 package (10 ounces) frozen peas and potatoes in cream sauce

1 cup milk

1 container (8 ounces) soft-style cream cheese

1 cup cubed cooked chicken or turkey

1 teaspoon chopped fresh or ¼ teaspoon dried basil leaves

Cook frozen peas and potatoes as directed on package, using 1½-quart saucepan. Meanwhile, heat milk and cream cheese in 1-quart saucepan over medium heat, stirring frequently, until cream cheese is melted. Stir cream cheese mixture into cooked pea mixture. Stir in chicken and basil; heat through. *2 servings.*

NUTRITION PER SERVING: Calories 675; Protein 39g; Carbohydrate 33g (Dietary Fiber 5g); Fat 45g (Unsaturated 18g, Saturated 27g); Cholesterol 190mg; Sodium 510mg.

PERCENT OF U.S. RDA: Vitamin A 46%; Vitamin C 10%; Calcium 28%; Iron 20%

Picante Chile

Shredded Cheddar cheese or sliced green onion sprinkled over the top will look pretty and taste great.

½ pound ground turkey or beef

1 can (15 ounces) chile beans in chile sauce, undrained

¾ cup picante sauce

¼ cup water

1 teaspoon chopped fresh cilantro or parsley

½ teaspoon sugar

Cook ground turkey in 1½-quart saucepan over medium heat, stirring frequently, until no longer pink. Stir in remaining ingredients. Heat to boiling; reduce heat. Cover and simmer about 10 minutes, stirring occasionally, until desired consistency. *2 servings.*

NUTRITION PER SERVING: Calories 365; Protein 33g; Carbohydrate 38g (Dietary Fiber 9g); Fat 13g (Unsaturated 9g, Saturated 4g); Cholesterol 75mg; Sodium 1840mg.

PERCENT OF U.S. RDA: Vitamin A 18%; Vitamin C 20%; Calcium 10%; Iron 32%

Southwestern Potato-Chicken Salad

(Photograph on page 91)

½ pint deli potato salad

6 ounces cut-up cooked chicken (about 1½ cups)

1 can (11 ounces) corn with red and green peppers, drained or 1½ cups frozen (thawed) corn with red peppers and broccoli

⅓ cup southwestern ranch dressing

1 tablespoon canned chopped green chiles

⅛ teaspoon ground cumin

Lettuce leaves

Gently mix all ingredients except lettuce. Serve on lettuce leaves. *2 servings.*

NUTRITION PER SERVING: Calories 595; Protein 31g; Carbohydrate 44g (Dietary Fiber 5g); Fat 35g (Unsaturated 29g, Saturated 6g); Cholesterol 95mg; Sodium 1220mg.

PERCENT OF U.S. RDA: Vitamin A 16%; Vitamin C 20%; Calcium 8%; Iron 14%

Turkey "Cranwiches"

2 slices (¾ ounces each) Colby, Monterey Jack or Cheddar cheese, cut into halves

¼ cup cranberry-orange sauce or relish

6 ounces thinly sliced cooked turkey

4 slices firm-textured wheat or rye bread

1 to 2 tablespoons margarine or butter, softened

Layer half each of the cheese, sauce and turkey on 2 slices bread. Top with remaining bread. Spread top slices of bread with about half of the margarine.

Place sandwiches, margarine side down, in 10-inch skillet. Spread top slices of bread with margarine. Cook uncovered over medium heat about 5 minutes or until golden brown. Turn and cook about 2 minutes longer or until golden brown and cheese is melted. *2 servings.*

NUTRITION PER SERVING: Calories 460; Protein 37g; Carbohydrate 41g (Dietary Fiber 3g); Fat 18g (Unsaturated 11g, Saturated 7g); Cholesterol 90mg; Sodium 570mg.

PERCENT OF U.S. RDA: Vitamin A 12%; Vitamin C *%; Calcium 18%; Iron 16%

TAILORED FOR TWO
Mix-and-Match-Salad-in-a-Sandwich Chart

Sandwiches are so easy to make for two, as well as portable and delicious. But sometimes we run out of ideas and keep serving the same old, plain old combinations. Turn the ho-hum into the sensational by using this chart. Select the amounts mentioned across the first three columns of meats, dressings and stir-ins, and serve it in or on one of the breads from the last column. *Each combination will make two sandwiches.*

Meats (choose 1)	Dressings (choose 1 or 2 to equal ¼ cup)	Stir-ins (choose 1 or 2)	Breads (choose 1)
¾ cup chopped cooked plain or smoked chicken or turkey	Mayonnaise or salad dressing (regular or reduced-calorie)	¼ cup chopped celery, bell pepper, seeded cucumber, tomatoes or water chestnuts	1 bagel, split
¾ cup chopped cooked roast beef, pork or smoked ham	Mayonnaise or salad dressing mixed with Dijon mustard (or dijon-mayonnaise blend) or prepared horseradish	¼ cup chopped apple or pear	1 large pita bread, cut into halves
¾ cup chopped pastrami, corned beef, salami or bologna		¼ cup shredded cheese, carrot or zucchini	2 large flour tortillas
3 hard-cooked eggs, chopped	Cream cheese, softened (regular or reduced-calorie) or plain or flavored whipped cream cheese	2 tablespoons sliced green onions, or chopped ripe or pimiento-stuffed olives or green chiles	2 hard or kaiser rolls, split
1 can (6 ounces) tuna, salmon or 1 can (4¼ ounces) shrimp, drained	Sour cream or plain yogurt	2 tablespoons raisins, dried cranberries or cherries, chopped dried apricots, or chopped nuts	2 English muffins, split
	Creamy bottled salad dressings such as Italian, Parmesan, Oriental-sesame, ranch or blue cheese, peppercorn, and nacho	2 slices bacon, crisply cooked and crumbled	2 rye hamburger buns
			4 slices raisin, whole wheat or pumpernickel bread
	Creamy dips such as sour cream-and-onion, dill, avocado		4 slices French bread, ½ inch thick

Apricot Fish

2 halibut or other lean fish steaks (about 8 ounces)

¼ cup apricot preserves

1 tablespoon white vinegar

¾ teaspoon chopped fresh or ¼ teaspoon dried tarragon leaves

Set oven control to broil. Grease broiler pan rack. Place fish steaks on rack in broiler pan. Broil with tops about 4 inches from heat 4 minutes. Turn fish; broil about 4 minutes longer or until fish flakes easily with fork. Mix remaining ingredients; spoon onto fish. Broil 1 minute longer. Serve any remaining apricot mixture with fish. *2 servings.*

NUTRITION PER SERVING: Calories 200; Protein 21g; Carbohydrate 25g (Dietary Fiber 0g); Fat 2g (Unsaturated 1g, Saturated 1g); Cholesterol 60mg; Sodium 110mg.

PERCENT OF U.S. RDA: Vitamin A *%; Vitamin C *%; Calcium 2%; Iron 4%

Parsleyed Parmesan Fish

(Photograph on page 92)

If you use frozen fish fillets, you'll find that the baking time will be closer to 16 minutes than to 12. The secret to cooking frozen fish to perfection is using a broiler pan that allows hot air to circulate evenly.

½ pound fresh or individually frozen (thawed) fish fillets

2 tablespoons grated Parmesan cheese

1 tablespoon Italian-style dry bread crumbs

1 tablespoon chopped fresh parsley

2 teaspoons margarine or butter, melted

Heat oven to 450°. Grease broiler pan rack. Place fish fillets in single layer on rack in broiler pan. Mix remaining ingredients; sprinkle over fish. Bake uncovered 12 to 16 minutes or until fish flakes easily with fork. *2 servings.*

NUTRITION PER SERVING: Calories 170; Protein 24g; Carbohydrate 3g (Dietary Fiber 0g); Fat 7g (Unsaturated 5g, Saturated 2g); Cholesterol 65mg; Sodium 250mg.

PERCENT OF U.S. RDA: Vitamin A 8%; Vitamin C *%; Calcium 8%; Iron 2%

Easy Fish and Vegetable Packets

2 frozen sole, perch or other lean fish fillets (about ½ pound)

2 cups frozen mixed broccoli, cauliflower and carrots

1½ teaspoons chopped fresh or ½ teaspoon dried dill weed

¼ teaspoon salt

⅛ teaspoon pepper

2 tablespoons dry white wine or chicken broth

Heat oven to 450°. Place each frozen fish fillet on 12-inch square of aluminum foil. Top each fillet with 1 cup of the vegetables. Sprinkle with dill weed, salt and pepper. Pour 1 tablespoon wine over each. Fold up sides of foil to make tent; fold top edges over to seal. Fold in sides, making a packet; fold to seal. Place packets on cookie sheet. Bake about 35 minutes or until vegetables are crisp-tender and fish flakes easily with fork. *2 servings.*

NUTRITION PER SERVING: Calories 140; Protein 24g; Carbohydrate 10g (Dietary Fiber 4g); Fat 2g (Unsaturated 1g, Saturated 1g); Cholesterol 60mg; Sodium 410mg.

PERCENT OF U.S. RDA: Vitamin A 100%; Vitamin C 34%; Calcium 6%; Iron 6%

Chutney-Salmon Salad

1 can (about 6 ounces) skinless, boneless salmon, drained and flaked

1½ cups broccoli slaw or coleslaw mix

⅓ cup mayonnaise or salad dressing

3 tablespoons chutney

¼ cup dry-roasted peanuts

Mix salmon, broccoli slaw, mayonnaise and chutney in glass or plastic bowl. Just before serving, stir in peanuts. *2 servings.*

NUTRITION PER SERVING: Calories 675; Protein 23g; Carbohydrate 20g (Dietary Fiber 3g); Fat 57g (Unsaturated 48g, Saturated 9g); Cholesterol 80mg; Sodium 990mg.

PERCENT OF U.S. RDA: Vitamin A 6%; Vitamin C 44%; Calcium 24%; Iron 10%

Shrimp-Pasta Salad Toss

(Photograph on page 93)

You can thin pasta salad from the deli by adding a tablespoon or two of milk, if needed.

6 ounces frozen cooked shrimp, thawed

2 cups bite-size pieces spinach

½ pint deli pasta salad

½ cup cherry tomatoes, cut into halves

2 tablespoons sliced pitted ripe olives

Toss all ingredients. *2 servings.*

NUTRITION PER SERVING: Calories 290; Protein 23g; Carbohydrate 25g (Dietary Fiber 3g); Fat 12g (Unsaturated 10g, Saturated 2g); Cholesterol 170mg; Sodium 860mg.

PERCENT OF U.S. RDA: Vitamin A 56%; Vitamin C 46%; Calcium 10%; Iron 30%

Herbed Fish Chowder

Frozen loose-pack hash browns most often come in nugget shapes and are also called potatoes O'Brien.

½ pound individually frozen fish fillets

1 cup frozen hash brown potatoes with onions and peppers

2 teaspoons chopped fresh or ¾ teaspoon dried marjoram leaves

⅛ teaspoon salt

⅛ teaspoon pepper

1 bottle (8 ounces) clam juice

1 can (12 ounces) evaporated milk

Mix all ingredients except milk in 1½-quart saucepan. Heat to boiling; reduce heat. Cover and simmer about 5 minutes, stirring and breaking up fish as it thaws, until fish flakes easily with fork and potatoes are tender. Stir in milk. Heat over medium heat, stirring frequently, until bubbly. *2 servings.*

NUTRITION PER SERVING: Calories 490; Protein 36g; Carbohydrate 35g (Dietary Fiber 2g); Fat 24g (Unsaturated 13g, Saturated 11g); Cholesterol 110mg; Sodium 990mg.

PERCENT OF U.S. RDA: Vitamin A 12%; Vitamin C *%; Calcium 48%; Iron 10%

Tuna-Slaw Pitas

½ pint deli coleslaw

1 can (6⅛ ounces) tuna in water, drained

1 tablespoon sunflower nuts

¼ to ½ teaspoon curry powder

*2 pita breads (6 inches in diameter), cut
crosswise into halves*

Mix coleslaw, tuna, sunflower nuts and curry powder. Fill pita bread halves with tuna mixture. *2 servings.*

NUTRITION PER SERVING: Calories 440; Protein 34g; Carbohydrate 52g (Dietary Fiber 3g); Fat 12g (Unsaturated 10g, Saturated 2g); Cholesterol 25mg; Sodium 860mg.

PERCENT OF U.S. RDA: Vitamin A 2%; Vitamin C 28%; Calcium 8%; Iron 28%

Crab-Dijon Sandwiches

*6 ounces frozen crabmeat or frozen salad-
style imitation crabmeat, thawed*

¼ cup mayonnaise or salad dressing

2 tablespoons grated Parmesan cheese

1 teaspoon Dijon mustard

2 English muffins, split and toasted

Set oven control to broil. Mix crabmeat, mayonnaise, cheese and mustard. Divide among muffin halves. Place on rack in broiler pan. Broil with tops 4 inches from heat 3 to 4 minutes or until tops start to brown. *2 servings.*

NUTRITION PER SERVING: Calories 430; Protein 23g; Carbohydrate 27g (Dietary Fiber 1g); Fat 26g (Unsaturated 21g, Saturated 5g); Cholesterol 100mg; Sodium 790mg.

PERCENT OF U.S. RDA: Vitamin A 2%; Vitamin C 4%; Calcium 24%; Iron 14%

Five-Spice Meatballs

A hearty meal is as easy as one, two, three dishes! While the meatballs are baking, prepare quick-cooking mashed potatoes and steam some green beans.

½ pound ground beef or pork

3 tablespoons fine dry bread crumbs

¼ teaspoon five-spice powder

1 egg white

¼ cup sweet-and-sour sauce

Heat oven to 375°. Mix ground beef, bread crumbs, five-spice powder and egg white. Shape mixture into 8 meatballs. Place in ungreased square pan, 18×8×2 inches. Bake about 20 minutes or until meatballs are no longer pink in center. Spoon sweet-and-sour sauce over meatballs. Bake 2 minutes longer. *2 servings.*

NUTRITION PER SERVING: Calories 310; Protein 21g; Carbohydrate 16g (Dietary Fiber 0g); Fat 18g (Unsaturated 11g, Saturated 7g); Cholesterol 70mg; Sodium 260mg.

PERCENT OF U.S. RDA: Vitamin A *%; Vitamin C *%; Calcium 2%; Iron 14%

Confetti Stroganoff

4 ounces uncooked egg noodles (about 2 cups)

½ pound ground pork or beef

¾ cup sour cream–and-onion dip

1 teaspoon all-purpose flour

2 tablespoons sliced ripe olives

1 jar (2 ounces) diced pimientos, drained

1 tablespoon chopped fresh parsley

Cook noodles as directed on package; drain. While noodles are cooking, cook ground pork in 1½-quart saucepan over medium heat about 5 minutes, stirring frequently, until brown; drain. Mix sour cream dip and flour; stir into pork. Stir in olives and pimientos. Cook, stirring constantly, until mixture is heated through (do not boil). Serve pork mixture over noodles. Sprinkle with parsley. *2 servings.*

NUTRITION PER SERVING: Calories 640; Protein 32g; Carbohydrate 43g (Dietary Fiber 3g); Fat 39g (Unsaturated 22g, Saturated 17g); Cholesterol 180mg; Sodium 1120mg.

PERCENT OF U.S. RDA: Vitamin A 12%; Vitamin C *%; Calcium 12%; Iron 20%

Raspberry-glazed Ham

1 fully cooked smoked ham slice, ½ inch thick (about ½ pound)

2 tablespoons raspberry spreadable fruit

2 teaspoons lemon juice

1 teaspoon chopped fresh or freeze-dried chives

1 teaspoon prepared mustard

Set oven control to broil. Cut outer edge of fat on ham slice diagonally at 1-inch intervals to prevent curling (do not cut into meat). Place ham on rack in broiler pan. Broil with top about 4 inches from heat about 5 minutes or until ham is heated through and has started to brown. Mix remaining ingredients; brush over ham. Broil 2 minutes longer. *2 servings.*

NUTRITION PER SERVING: Calories 295; Protein 23g; Carbohydrate 13g (Dietary Fiber 0g); Fat 17g (Unsaturated 11g, Saturated 6g); Cholesterol 70mg; Sodium 1110mg.

PERCENT OF U.S. RDA: Vitamin A *%; Vitamin C 10%; Calcium 2%; Iron 10%

Italian Kabobs

(*Photograph on page 94*)

½ pound fully cooked Polish sausage, cut into 1-inch pieces

½ small green bell pepper, cut into 1-inch pieces

8 medium whole mushrooms

¼ cup creamy Italian or creamy garlic dressing

4 cherry tomatoes

Set oven control to broil. Thread sausage pieces, bell pepper pieces and mushrooms alternately on each of four 10- or 11-inch skewers,* leaving space between each piece. Place kabobs on rack in broiler pan. Brush half of the dressing over kabobs.

Broil kabobs with tops about 4 inches from heat 5 minutes; turn. Add tomato to end of each skewer. Brush kabobs with remaining dressing. Broil about 5 minutes longer or until bell pepper pieces are crisp-tender. *2 servings.*

* If using bamboo skewers, soak in water at least 30 minutes before using to prevent burning.

NUTRITION PER SERVING: Calories 525; Protein 17g; Carbohydrate 9g (Dietary Fiber 1g); Fat 47g (Unsaturated 33g, Saturated 14g); Cholesterol 80mg; Sodium 1230mg.

PERCENT OF U.S. RDA: Vitamin A 20%; Vitamin C 10%; Calcium 2%; Iron 14%

QUICK-TO-FIX IDEAS

When you feel pressed for time, it can be hard to come up with super-easy, super-quick dishes. The ideas here prove that delicious main dishes, sides, salads and desserts can be ready in just minutes. Suggestions range from kid-perfect snacks to elegant desserts for a candlelit dinner. Try a few of these delicious ideas; they'll be ready to eat in no time at all.

Super Snacks and Appetizers

- Fix a quick mini pizza, using tortillas, bagels, English muffins, crackers, rice cakes or hard rolls as the crust. Spread with pizza sauce and your favorite toppings, then microwave or broil in a toaster oven or regular oven.

- Spread peanut butter or softened cream cheese (plain or flavored) on fruit and vegetable slices.

- Brush saltine crackers or tortilla chips with melted margarine or butter and sprinkle with cinnamon-sugar. Bake until bubbly; cool slightly before eating.

- Split leftover biscuits, popovers or croissants and top with shredded cheese and chopped green chiles. Broil or bake until the cheese is melted.

- Purchase already cleaned and cut-up vegetables in the produce section to use for dipping, and hard-cooked eggs from the deli to make deviled eggs.

Marvelous Main Dishes

- Add a small can (4 ounces) of tuna or chicken to a single serving size can of soup (8 ounces).

- Use canned or frozen shrimp or crab in stir-fry dishes. Combine with deli or leftover vegetables and teriyaki sauce.

- Prepare frozen chicken or turkey patties as directed on package. Top with spaghetti sauce and mozzarella cheese. Bake or broil until cheese is melted.

- Place two skinless boneless chicken breasts in a small plastic bag. Add your favorite salad dressing or sauce (Italian dressing, barbecue sauce, vinaigrette dressing or teriyaki sauce). Press out the air, seal the bag and marinate overnight in the refrigerator. Remove from the bag and broil or microwave.

- Keep frozen cooked meatballs and prepared spaghetti sauce on hand to heat quickly and serve over your favorite pasta.

- Grill extra steaks, chops or burgers to reheat later in the microwave (or freeze and reheat).

- Buy cooked meats by the chunk, sliced from the deli or chopped from the salad bar to use in casseroles, salads or sandwiches.

- Create a quick bean burger: spread buns with mayonnaise. Top with baked beans and shredded cheese. Broil until the cheese melts.

Pasta, Rice and Potatoes on the Side

- Dress up hot cooked rice by stirring in shredded cheese and chopped green onion or chopped green chiles.

- Make quick Mexican rice by stirring mild or hot salsa into hot cooked rice—about ¼ cup salsa per 1 cup of rice.

- Stir-fry leftover pasta in olive oil and garlic until hot. Sprinkle with grated Parmesan cheese before serving.

- Brush ¼- to ½-inch slices of leftover baked potato with melted margarine or butter and top with grated Parmesan cheese. Broil until the cheese is lightly browned.

- Microwave sweet potatoes and top with butter and a sprinkling of brown sugar and cinnamon.

Vegetables and Salads

- Toss hot cooked vegetables with your favorite prepared sauce (teriyaki, barbecue, taco), bottled salad dressing (Italian, creamy peppercorn or Parmesan) or a dab of your favorite mustard such as Dijon.

- Just before vegetables are done, drain and stir in cheese spread. Cover and let stand a few minutes until hot. Stir in a little milk if cheese is too thick.

- Mix and match your favorite greens with the vegetables and other "extras" offered at the salad bar of your favorite supermarket. Try a new combination each time.

- Purchase packaged cleaned mixed greens— half the package is just right for two. Toss the greens with hot vinaigrette dressing, then top with thinly sliced grilled chicken, beef or pork.

- For super salad toppers, try nuts, broken crackers, unsweetened ready-to-eat breakfast cereal or crunchy chow mein noodles instead of croutons.

Simply Delicious Desserts

- Make fruit-topped cookie tarts by spreading large cookies with frosting or softened cream cheese and topping with fresh fruit or all-fruit preserves.

- Sprinkle thin slices of purchased pound cake or angel food cake with chocolate chips and miniature marshmallows. Broil about 5 inches from heat about 1 minute or until marshmallows are golden.

- Toast frozen waffle squares and top with warm fruit pie filling and whipped cream or ice cream.

- For a quick caramel apple sundae, thinly slice an apple and top with caramel ice cream topping and toasted nuts. Delicious with or without the ice cream!

- Add a special twist to your favorite ice cream, sherbet or frozen yogurt by using purchased toppings or liqueurs in interesting combinations. Top coffee ice cream with white chocolate sauce; chocolate ice cream with maple syrup; pineapple sherbet with sherry wine; orange sherbet with hot fudge sauce; vanilla frozen yogurt with cranberry liqueur; and raspberry frozen yogurt with apricot preserves mixed with rum. Serve with crisp cookies.

Gyros-style Lamb Chops

Remember this tangy topper the next time you need to dress up pork chops or burgers.

> *2 lamb loin chops, 1 inch thick (about ½ pound)*
>
> *1 teaspoon margarine or butter*
>
> *2 tablespoons chopped onion*
>
> *2 tablespoons plain yogurt or sour cream*
>
> *2 tablespoons creamy cucumber dressing*

Set oven control to broil. Cut outer edge of fat on lamb chops diagonally at 1-inch intervals to prevent curling (do not cut into meat). Grease broiler pan rack. Place lamb chops on rack in broiler pan. Broil with tops about 5 inches from heat about 6 minutes or until brown; turn. Broil 9 to 10 minutes longer for medium doneness (160°).

Meanwhile, heat margarine in 1-quart saucepan over medium heat until melted. Cook onion in margarine about 2 minutes, stirring frequently, until tender. Mix onion mixture, yogurt and dressing; serve over lamb. *2 servings.*

NUTRITION PER SERVING: Calories 385; Protein 22g; Carbohydrate 4g (Dietary Fiber 0g); Fat 31g (Unsaturated 20g, Saturated 11g); Cholesterol 90mg; Sodium 260mg.

PERCENT OF U.S. RDA: Vitamin A 4%; Vitamin C *%; Calcium 6%; Iron 10%

Quick Beef and Vegetable Soup

> *½ pound ground beef or pork*
>
> *1 cup frozen mixed broccoli, cauliflower and carrots*
>
> *¼ cup uncooked shell or elbow macaroni*
>
> *2 cups water*
>
> *1 tablespoon beef bouillon granules*
>
> *½ teaspoon Italian seasoning*

Cook ground beef in 1½-quart saucepan over medium heat, stirring frequently, until brown; drain. Stir in remaining ingredients. Heat to boiling; reduce heat. Cover and simmer about 15 minutes, stirring occasionally, until macaroni is tender. *2 servings.*

NUTRITION PER SERVING: Calories 320; Protein 23g; Carbohydrate 19g (Dietary Fiber 2g); Fat 18g (Unsaturated 11g, Saturated 7g); Cholesterol 70mg; Sodium 2000mg.

PERCENT OF U.S. RDA: Vitamin A 50%; Vitamin C 10%; Calcium 2%; Iron 16%

Sausage-Lentil Soup

> *1 cup water*
>
> *¼ cup dried lentils, sorted and rinsed*
>
> *½ pound bulk Italian sausage*
>
> *1 can (8 ounces) stewed tomatoes*
>
> *1 can (5½ ounces) spicy eight-vegetable juice*
>
> *1 teaspoon chopped fresh or ¼ teaspoon dried rosemary leaves*

Heat water and lentils to boiling in 1-quart saucepan; reduce heat. Cover and simmer about 25 minutes, stirring occasionally, until lentils are tender.

Meanwhile, cook sausage in 1½-quart saucepan over medium heat, stirring frequently, until brown; drain. Stir in remaining ingredients. Heat to boiling; reduce heat. Cover and simmer 15 minutes, stirring occasionally. Stir in undrained lentils; heat through. *2 servings.*

NUTRITION PER SERVING: Calories 515; Protein 31g; Carbohydrate 32g (Dietary Fiber 6g); Fat 32g (Unsaturated 21g, Saturated 11g); Cholesterol 90mg; Sodium 1640mg.

PERCENT OF U.S. RDA: Vitamin A 20%; Vitamin C 50%; Calcium 6%; Iron 30%

Zucchini-Beef Sandwiches

1 tablespoon margarine or butter

1 small zucchini, shredded

½ teaspoon Italian seasoning

6 ounces thinly sliced cooked roast beef

*1 pita bread (6 inches in diameter), cut
  crosswise into halves*

Heat margarine in 10-inch skillet over medium heat until melted. Cook zucchini and Italian seasoning in margarine about 2 minutes, stirring frequently, until zucchini is tender. Add roast beef, spooning some of the zucchini mixture over beef. Cover and simmer about 2 minutes or until beef is heated through. Fill pita bread halves with zucchini mixture. *2 servings.*

NUTRITION PER SERVING: Calories 465; Protein 23g; Carbohydrate 26g (Dietary Fiber 2g); Fat 31g (Unsaturated 20g, Saturated 11g); Cholesterol 70mg; Sodium 330mg.

PERCENT OF U.S. RDA: Vitamin A 8%; Vitamin C 4%; Calcium 4%; Iron 16%

Zesty Barbecue Sandwiches

Serve these sandwiches with baked beans and coleslaw and you can have a mini "barbecue" any time of year.

½ cup ketchup

1 tablespoon orange marmalade

½ teaspoon chile powder

*6 ounces thinly sliced cooked roast beef
  or pork*

*2 kaiser rolls or hamburger buns, split
  and toasted*

Mix ketchup, orange marmalade and chili powder in 1-quart saucepan. Cover and cook over low heat 5 minutes, stirring occasionally. Stir in roast beef. Cover and cook over low heat 5 minutes, stirring occasionally. Fill rolls with beef mixture. *2 servings.*

NUTRITION PER SERVING: Calories 545; Protein 25g; Carbohydrate 53g (Dietary Fiber 3g); Fat 27g (Unsaturated 16g, Saturated 11g); Cholesterol 75mg; Sodium 1090mg.

PERCENT OF U.S. RDA: Vitamin A 8%; Vitamin C *%; Calcium 4%; Iron 22%

Feta-stuffed Lamb Patties

(*Photograph on page 95*)

½ pound ground lamb or beef

2 tablespoons crumbled feta cheese

2 tablespoons sour cream

1 tablespoon pesto

2 hamburger buns, split and toasted

Set oven control to broil. Shape ground lamb into 4 thin patties, about 4 inches in diameter. Place 1 tablespoon of the cheese on each of 2 patties. Top with remaining patties, pressing edges to seal in cheese. Place patties on rack in broiler pan. Broil with tops about 4 inches from heat 6 to 7 minutes on each side until lamb is no longer pink in center.

Mix sour cream and pesto. Place patties on bottoms of buns. Top with pesto mixture and tops of buns. *2 servings.*

NUTRITION PER SERVING: Calories 405; Protein 22g; Carbohydrate 24g (Dietary Fiber 1g); Fat 25g (Unsaturated 14g, Saturated 11g); Cholesterol 90mg; Sodium 400mg.

PERCENT OF U.S. RDA: Vitamin A 2%; Vitamin C *%; Calcium 14%; Iron 14%

Sunshine Frittata

If you don't have an ovenproof nonstick skillet, wrap the handle of your regular skillet in a double thickness of aluminum foil and add an extra tablespoon of margarine before pouring in the egg mixture. For extra flavor, add ¼ teaspoon chopped fresh mint or dill weed.

4 eggs

¼ cup milk

⅛ teaspoon salt

½ cup shredded provolone or mozzarella cheese (2 ounces)

1 tablespoon margarine or butter

½ cup shredded carrot

Beat eggs, milk and salt in medium bowl until blended. Stir in cheese. Heat margarine in 8-inch ovenproof nonstick skillet over medium heat until melted. Cook carrot in margarine about 3 minutes, stirring frequently, until tender; reduce heat to medium-low. Pour egg mixture over carrots. Cover and cook about 7 minutes, without stirring, until eggs are set almost to center and are light brown on bottom. Remove cover.

Set oven control to broil. Broil frittata with top about 5 inches from heat about 2 minutes or until eggs are completely set and just starting to brown. *2 servings.*

NUTRITION PER SERVING: Calories 325; Protein 21g; Carbohydrate 7g (Dietary Fiber 1g); Fat 24g (Unsaturated 14g, Saturated 10g); Cholesterol 450mg; Sodium 640mg.

PERCENT OF U.S. RDA: Vitamin A 100%; Vitamin C *%; Calcium 30%; Iron 10%

Blue Cheese Quesadillas

(Photograph on page 96)

These unusual quesadillas make terrific party appetizers.

Peach Salsa (page 16)

½ cup shredded Monterey Jack cheese (2 ounces)

¼ cup soft-style cream cheese

3 tablespoons chopped walnuts

2 tablespoons crumbled blue cheese

1 green onion, sliced

4 flour tortillas (6 inches in diameter)

Prepare Peach Salsa. Heat oven to 375°. Grease cookie sheet. Mix remaining ingredients except tortillas. Place two tortillas on cookie sheet and spread with cheese mixture. Top with remaining tortillas. Bake 8 to 10 minutes or until cheese begins to melt and tortillas start to brown. Cut into wedges and serve with Peach Salsa. *2 servings.*

NUTRITION PER SERVING: Calories 550; Protein 18g; Carbohydrate 53g (Dietary Fiber 3g); Fat 31g (Unsaturated 16g, Saturated 15g); Cholesterol 60mg; Sodium 990mg.

PERCENT OF U.S. RDA: Vitamin A 18%; Vitamin C *%; Calcium 34%; Iron 24%

METRIC CONVERSION GUIDE

U.S. UNITS	CANADIAN METRIC	AUSTRALIAN METRIC
Volume		
1/4 teaspoon	1 mL	1 ml
1/2 teaspoon	2 mL	2 ml
1 teaspoon	5 mL	5 ml
1 tablespoon	15 mL	20 ml
1/4 cup	50 mL	60 ml
1/3 cup	75 mL	80 ml
1/2 cup	125 mL	125 ml
2/3 cup	150 mL	170 ml
3/4 cup	175 mL	190 ml
1 cup	250 mL	250 ml
1 quart	1 liter	1 liter
1 1/2 quarts	1.5 liter	1.5 liter
2 quarts	2 liters	2 liters
2 1/2 quarts	2.5 liters	2.5 liters
3 quarts	3 liters	3 liters
4 quarts	4 liters	4 liters
Weight		
1 ounce	30 grams	30 grams
2 ounces	55 grams	60 grams
3 ounces	85 grams	90 grams
4 ounces (1/4 pound)	115 grams	125 grams
8 ounces (1/2 pound)	225 grams	225 grams
16 ounces (1 pound)	455 grams	500 grams
1 pound	455 grams	1/2 kilogram

Measurements		**Temperatures**	
Inches	Centimeters	Fahrenheit	Celsius
1	2.5	32°	0°
2	5.0	212°	100°
3	7.5	250°	120°
4	10.0	275°	140°
5	12.5	300°	150°
6	15.0	325°	160°
7	17.5	350°	180°
8	20.5	375°	190°
9	23.0	400°	200°
10	25.5	425°	220°
11	28.0	450°	230°
12	30.5	475°	240°
13	33.0	500°	260°
14	35.5		
15	38.0		

NOTE
The recipes in this cookbook have not been developed or tested using metric measures. When converting recipes to metric, some variations in quality may be noted.

INDEX